Love Him, Hate Him:

Ten Years of Sports, Passion, and Kansas City

■

by Jason Whitlock

Kansas City Star Books

Acknowledgements:

This book is dedicated to the many people who have helped me along the way. It's impossible to accomplish much in life without the support of good people. I've been surrounded by good people. In no particular order, I want to thank Bob Hammel, Andy Graham, Dale Bye, Mike Fannin, Jeff Sheran, Rob Lanessey, Chad Boeger, Ollie Gates, Scott Cruce, Damon Ferbrache, Carol Coe, Lawrence Cooley, Jerry Stauffer, Lee Dilk, Joe Valerio, Mike Lupica, Bob Wojnowski, Neal Scarbrough, Kevin Jackson, Mike Weinstein, Geoff Larcom, Kirk and Susie May, Matt Nevinger and my family.

Love Him, Hate Him
10 Years of Sports, Passion and Kansas City

By Jason Whitlock

Editor: Matt Nevinger
Cover photograph: Gregory Booker
Design: Vicky Frenkel

First edition.
ISBN: 0-9754804-6-4
Printed in the United States of America by Walsworth Publishing Co., Marceline, Missouri

To order copies, call StarInfo at (816) 234-4636 and say "BOOKS."
Order on-line at www.TheKansasCityStore.com.

✳ KANSAS CITY STAR BOOKS

When this project was first conceived Ralph Wiley agreed to write the introduction. However, on June 13, 2004 Wiley died of heart failure at his home in Orlando. This book is dedicated to his memory.

Ralph Wiley
April 12, 1952—June 13, 2004

TABLE OF CONTENTS

Once Upon a Time You Just Had to Be Good: The Influence and Evolution of Big Business and Sports

The Forward Pass Was Not the Most Important Innovation of the Last Century: The Media and Its Impact on Sports

Yes It's Serious, But That Doesn't Mean You Can't Laugh: Sometimes Sports Are Just Fun

The Chiefs Will Go 16-0: Bold Predictions from the Last Decade...Some of Which Were Accurate

In the Moment, Part 1: The Success, Achievements, and Accomplishments of the Last 10 Years

It Doesn't Always Stay on the Field: Race, Gender, and Politics in the World of Sports

In the Moment, Part 2: The Greatest Disappointments and Tragedies of the Last Decade

I WANNA BE LIKE MIKE

My dad has always read the newspaper cover to cover first thing every morning. He grabs the morning rag, takes it to the bathroom and devours the words of the writers for the Indianapolis Star. He hates the Indy Star. Always has. He thinks it's biased and racist and uninformed. But he reads it every day, start to finish, because it's the best source of daily information he's ever found.

I fell in love/hate with the Indianapolis Star when I was seven or eight. My relationship with my hometown news-paper was a byproduct of my love affair with the Indiana Pacers. Back then, long before the Internet, long before sports-talk radio, long before ESPN, the Indy Star was the only place to follow the progress of the Pacers, champions of the red-white-blue ABA.

Reading about Darnell Hillman, Roger Brown, Mel Daniels, Don Buse and Slick Leonard gave me a reason to wake up each morning. After my parents divorced, my mother kept a subscription to the Indianapolis Star primari-ly so I could follow my Pacers. I'd wake each morning by 6, stumble to the front door of our three-bedroom apart-ment and spread out the sports section in the middle of our living-room floor.

In 1976, after the ABA folded, the Pacers joined the NBA and quickly established themselves as one of the worst professional sports organizations in the history of organized athletics. Things once got so bad for my Pacers that they were forced to hold a Jerry Lewis-like telethon to keep their operation afloat. It was during this tragic era of Pacers bas-ketball that my relationship with my hometown newspaper turned from love to hate.

The Indy Star's soft, "homer-ish" coverage of my sad-sack Pacers infuriated me. I read the newspaper every day hoping that the people responsible for ruining my beloved team would be held accountable. When former Pacers coach George Irvine insisted on turning Wayman Tisdale, the best back-to-the-basket, low-post scorer I'd ever seen, into a face-the-basket, put-the-ball-on-the-floor small forward, I couldn't sleep at night. I'd wake each morning fantasizing about a newspaper column that would call for Irvine's immediate resignation and mental-hospitalization.

Morning after morning, all I read was excuses and rationalizations and wait-til-next-year optimism.

Seeking an alternative, I asked my mother to get a second newspaper subscription. We ordered the afternoon paper, the Indianapolis News. To my great disappointment, the News' coverage of the Pacers was nothing more than re-warmed versions of the same garbage I'd read in the morning.

I later accidentally discovered the one major advantage The News held over The Star: Mike Royko, the celebrated and Pulitzer Prize-winning Chicago-based columnist.

Three times a week, in its A section, the Indianapolis News ran Royko's nationally-syndicated column. I can't remember the first Royko column I ever read. I just remember being severely disappointed on the days his columns didn't run. Royko was opinionated, irreverent, insightful, brash and free of nagging agendas. Royko pissed everyone off — Republicans, Democrats, conservatives, liberals, blacks, whites, men, women, mayors, aldermen, friends and foes —

and would sporadically make everyone happy.

Halfway through my freshman year at Ball State University, when a friend suggested that I switch my major to journalism, I told myself that I wanted to be like Mike — Royko, not Jordan. I wanted to write an agenda-free, personal column. I wanted to write a column that was worthy of newspaper publication rather than publication in "the paper," a newspaper that values words more than news and insight. I wanted to write a column that celebrated a city's victories and critically analyzed a city's failures. I wanted to make people laugh and cry. I wanted to be a slave to common sense, not a slave to a particular ideology. I wanted to write my version of the truth. It's impossible for one man or woman to identify the absolute truth. All we can do is tell our version. Royko told his version artfully and passionately and in a crisp, no-nonsense, plain-spoken style. The truths Royko spewed stood up over time because he was uncompromised.

I hope some of the things I've written over the past 10 years still ring true today and tomorrow.

Jason

When Jason Came to Kansas City

by Buck O'Neil

People in Kansas City weren't ready for Jason when he first got here. The people weren't accustomed to his style, he didn't sound like what they had heard before. Jason tells it like it is, and he can get right down on the high school kid's level and he can get right on the level with the PhD. When he got to Kansas City he said things people were afraid of. It was different.

But Kansas City adjusted to Jason. Good thing too, because Jason is Jason and that wasn't going to change. He has a lot to offer and he has educated us to the truth; the way it is, not the way you want it to be. It is so important to have that truth, and when you're around Jason you'd better tell it just like it is. If you don't, he'll catch you. Sometimes people don't like the truth and they don't want to hear it. Jason says just what it is. It can make people mad, but it's the right way.

I don't think Jason's changed since he came here. He's the same guy. He's matured, but he's the same guy. He's good for Kansas City because he's from the Midwest.

Indianapolis is a lot like Kansas City. New York, Chicago, Los Angeles, those are all different. The Midwest is family; people come together here. Other places can be hard but in Kansas City if you do things right people will support it.

People may not realize it, but Jason brings us together. He makes us talk. He makes us talk honestly. The good book says "the truth will set you free." Jason's column sometimes sets us free to talk about things we'd rather avoid. You can't avoid the truth forever. If the Royals stink, Jason will say it. If the Chiefs stink, he'll say that, too. And if Jason thinks someone is doing something that will hurt Kansas City – and it doesn't matter who it is — Jason will go after them.

Jason's a good young man and he's good for this city. We've got a lot of great things here, and Jason in his way is trying to make things better. To get ahead, sometimes you have to have that guy who isn't afraid to say what's on his mind, to say what he thinks is right. It may not be popular. But it's what he believes is right. Jason stands for something. He won't fall. And if he does, he'll get right back up.

Chapter 1

Good Friends Talk
About More than Just Sports:
Personal Tales

Let's make this a good friendship

October 2, 1994

Jason's first column for The Kansas City Star reads even better now than it did when it first appeared. A column that truly stands the test of time.

I'm the reason the Chiefs lost last Sunday.

The loss had little to do with the Chiefs' offensive line getting whipped or Joe Montana's interceptions or Marty's aversion to field goals.

Nope, it was me.

If my two-year stop in Michigan taught me anything, it was to blame myself when a calamity struck the local populace.

The Chiefs were riding high until I got here, just six days before the Los Angeles Lams invaded America's heartland and destroyed the Chiefs 16-0.

I apologize.

That apology will have to suffice for all future Chiefs or Royals or Wildcats or Jayhawks or Tigers failures. There will be no more apologies (at least for failures I played no part in). Only opinions, insight, candor, irreverence and sometimes, I hope, humor will spew from my sports-saturated brain to my stubby fingers.

I'm your new columnist. I hope we can establish a mutually enjoyable relationship. I have to admit my record isn't good when it comes to long-term commitments usually my, uh, honesty gets in the way of the mutually enjoyable aspect of a relationship, or so I have been told by the kinder, gentler, whinier gender.

But I always enter each relationship hoping that "this is the one." And that is how I begin this new endeavor, believing that you — Star readers — and I will spend the rest of our lives together, sharing the lowlights and the highlights of the sporting world, satisfying each others' needs and second-guessing players, coaches, executives, and, yes, even decaying, Hall of Fame quarterbacks. And I'm not talking about Len Dawson.

It's always best to start a relationship by disclosing pertinent information to your partner. So I must tell you that I have been tested for rudeness, negativity, cheapshottivity, cynicism and the ability to jump off slow-moving bandwagons.

And according to my doctor the results are positive.

I arrived in KC after a short stay in Ann Arbor, a liberal bastion where every April Fools' Day police surround an entire park to protect Kato Kaelin lookalikes participating in Hash Bash, a marijuana smoke-off that rappers Dr. Dre, Snoop Doggy Dogg and Da Brat would be proud of.

Ann Arbor's also the home of the University of Michigan, where basketball players tell coaches what to do and football players invent ways to blow national championships.

I'm a bit of a rabble-rouser.

I launched my most successful cause from Ann Arbor. I founded the We Be Wantin' Magic Off Da Air Foundation, a non-profit corporation with the single purpose of ridding the TV airwaves of Magic Johnson's mush-mouthed NBA analysis.

I've also lived in Charlotte, N.C., and Bloomington, Ind., where I learned basketball at the foot (it was on my neck) of The General, Bobby Knight, the greatest coach in all the world and a really, really nice guy once you get past his bad breath, overall rudeness and megalomaniac tendencies.

I was born and reared in Indianapolis. My dream was to be a professional football player, and — in my opinion — I was an offensive lineman ahead of my time, a guy who played with just as much butt as guts. Or is that as much gut as butts?

Whatever, I was the original Nate Newton, the Dallas Cowboy All-Pro guard who appears to be headed both directions. My coaches at Ball State never quite saw it that way, though.

But enough reminiscing about the good ol' days. It's time to ponder the beginning of our wonderful relationship.

Please. I'm begging you. Respect me in the morning.

Marathon training no picnic
October 19, 2002

Jason only made it 5 miles in his first marathon. But he was greeted at the five-mile marker by an Ollie Gates Presidential Platter. He made it 11 miles in his second marathon but there was no Presidential Platter.

My body hurts. All of it, my knees, my ankles, my back, my hips, my neck, my feet, my butt, my brain. Massages don't help much. Two hours in a hot tub aren't much relief. I'm sick, coming down with the flu.

Writing a column for The Star and ESPN.com, being a host of a radio show, traveling to games, second-guessing Greg Robinson, arguing with James Hasty, jetting to New York for a TV show, serving as spokesman for Big Brothers Big Sisters of Greater Kansas City, piecing together a personal life and mixing in some daily marathon training takes a toll on a man, particularly when without your knowledge you've been selected Kansas City's No. 1 food taster by KC's Restaurant Owners Association.

The Humana River Crown Plaza Marathon is exactly two weeks from today, and guess who feels as if he's spent the last eight months wrestling Will Shields, Willie Roaf, John Tait, Casey Wiegmann and Brian Waters for the last pork chop at a tailgate party?

I knew training for a marathon would be the most difficult athletic challenge of my life. I knew I would have to be disciplined and determined. I knew my schedule would make it rough.

What I didn't know is that every restaurant owner and manager in Kansas City would take it upon himself to prove to me that their ribs are better than Ollie Gates'. What I didn't know is that every soccer mom, doughnut shop and wannabe chef would join the battle to prove they could make a dessert better than my mom's pound cake.

Let me make this clear: No one barbecues better than Mr. Gates. And, with apologies to my Aunt Mae; America's No. 1 soccer mom, Susie May; and Neil Smith's mom, no one cooks better than my mama.

Death, taxes, Mr. Gates on the grill and my mama in the kitchen — those are life's certainties.

Kansas City, I'm begging you, quit feeding me. Treat me like the bear in the zoo. You can fantasize about what my jaws would look like munching on the slab of spare ribs you marinated overnight and slow-roasted for four hours, but don't force them on my plate. It's dangerous, and it's going to be costly for me come Nov. 2.

I'm living up to my pledge. I'll be at the start line at 7:30 a.m. Nov. 2. I plan on walking (I never said I was running the marathon) as far as I can for as long as I can. I've been led to believe I have eight hours. I'm going to use them all.

When it's over, I'm going to write a check to the Community Blood Center. I'm donating $250 for every mile I don't complete of the 26-mile course. The Star is going to donate $250 for every mile I do complete.

And after I spend a week in traction, I'm going to get up and start preparing for the 2003 Humana River Crown Plaza Marathon. I'm going to walk this marathon (and donate money to the charity benefactor) every year until I complete it in less than six hours.

Even though there have been many snags in the road, I've absolutely enjoyed the experience of training and talking to die-hard runners and people who took up the marathon challenge after hearing I took the plunge. When I got involved with the marathon I had no idea how big KC's running community is. Al Saunders, the Chiefs' offensive coordinator, is a passionate runner who spent 15 minutes with me one day sharing his ideas on how we can make Kansas City's marathon the most fun and festive in the country.

I want to help do that. Nov. 2 is just the start of something we can really make big. I want you to join me in two weeks at Barney Allis Plaza, 12th and Baltimore. We start there. Even if you haven't been training, you can walk with me. Trust me, I'll be moving very slowly. Or you can do the 5-kilometer or half-marathon. The marathon also still needs about 50 volunteers to help with the race.

If you've cooked something you'd like for me to taste, check back with me in 2004.

Soul of my family will be missed
November 23, 1999

This column speaks for itself.

God gave her the perfect name. Lovie Kennedy. We called her Mama Lovie.

She was my grandmother, the foundation and the soul of my family.

She fell sick a couple of weeks ago. Sunday morning at the age of 83, she died in her sleep. A piece of me went with her.

Mama Lovie taught me everything I know about love, compassion and forgiveness. She epitomized unconditional love and unlimited forgiveness. She loved everyone. She forgave everyone.

When she was just a child a Ku Klux Klan lynch mob ran her family out of the South at gunpoint. They barged into her home, fired shots, grabbed her father and carried him outside for hanging. My great-grandfather avoided lynching by signaling that he was a Mason.

He packed his family up and left Kentucky for Indianapolis.

For many years after that my grandmother had an excessive fear of and hatred for white people. But midway through her life her love of God conquered her fear and hatred.

"Jesus took all my anger and bitterness and racism away," she'd say. "We're all the same in Jesus' eyes."

I can't ever remember Mama Lovie saying a bad word about anybody, other than the devil. I can't ever remember anyone saying a bad word about Mama Lovie. She had more friends than — as she would say — "Carter had liver pills."

You might be wondering why a sports columnist is writing a story about his grandmother.

I'm writing about her because as I've thought about Mama Lovie the last two weeks, I've wondered what my life would be like if I'd never known her.

She gave me my religious foundation. I spent a good part of each summer with her attending vacation Bible school. It was at her house that I decided to be baptized.

The first year I played football, she carried me back and forth to practice. She was my team's most enthusiastic cheerleader. She loved to talk football with me. She called me every year right in the middle of the Super Bowl. She talked away my tears the year my beloved Los Angeles

Rams lost to the Pittsburgh Steelers in the Super Bowl.

As I got older, I leaned on her wisdom and faith more and more. I can remember an overnight discussion in my college dorm room about religion. I called Mama Lovie at 3 a.m. and asked her opinion about what we were discussing.

The summer before my junior year of college we lived together. My father and I fell out over my immaturity. I packed my bags and moved into Mama Lovie's small, one-bedroom apartment in the 'hood.

She had two twin beds in her bedroom. We both snored. We'd talk well into the night about God, commitment to family, marriage, parenting and what I wanted to eat the next day. It was one of the best experiences of my life.

The wisdom she shared with me that summer sticks with me to this day. She taught me to use my faith in God as a weapon and shield against racism. From her I learned about the importance of sacrifice, particularly when it comes to helping your family.

I guess I'm writing about Mama Lovie because some days sports seem rather insignificant. I wonder whether we realize how few days we actually get on this earth, how little time we get to spend with the Mama Lovies. The Chiefs lost a third straight game Sunday, and this city fell into a deep depression Sunday night and Monday morning.

I'm fairly young. I have virtually no experience in dealing with the death of someone close to me. Many of the things that were important to me seem rather trivial now that Mama Lovie is gone.

■

George worthy of consideration
October 10, 1996

Jason's love affair with Jeff George is about the only hole in Jason's game. But George's loyalty to Jason is as strong as Jason's loyalty to his former high school teammate George. Jason wanted the Chiefs to sign George more than Jason wanted to share a short end with Halle Berry.

So that we're all on the same page, let me first admit that I'm biased when it comes to Jeff George, the suspended, rifle-armed quarterback of the Atlanta Falcons.

Growing up we shared the same neighborhood and won a high school state football championship together, and the guy comes from one of the most loyal and loving families I've ever seen.

So that we remain on the same page, let me add that I pride myself on being honest about people I care about and have a predisposed disposition to like.

If anyone cares to remember, in one of my first columns upon arriving here, I pointed out the poor work habits of my mother — whom I love dearly and to whom I am forever indebted for her many sacrifices — and her union-backed, too-powerful co-workers.

OK. Are we all on the same page?

What you're about to read is the truth about George, the quarterback who could help the Chiefs reach the Super Bowl, save Paul Hackett's behind and allow Steve Bono to return to his rightful place as a No. 2 quarterback.

George and I chatted for about 45 minutes Wednesday afternoon. We talked about many things, but we spent most of our time discussing his desire to move to a stable, classy, well-run organization.

I told him I knew of such an organization. But I added that the King of that organization and all of the King's disciples

didn't know the truth about Jeff George. So here it is.
Jeff George is not Roberto Alomar. George isn't Michael
Irvin. And he isn't the whiny, malcontented bum that the
national news media is making him out to be.

Since high school, George's football career has been marred
by his naive and loyal nature. He comes from a family that
wears its heart and its loyalty on its sleeves, pants legs and
shoes.

That's what led to his on-field blow-up with Atlanta Coach
June Jones. But before I deal with that much-overblown
incident, let me go back to the beginning. Let me explain in
detail what happened to George at Purdue, the University of
Miami, Illinois, the Indianapolis Colts and finally in Atlanta.

George was the 1985 national high school football player of
the year. Every major college in the country coveted his
services.

He made a bad decision choosing Purdue. The Boilermakers
were in the process of falling apart. George chose Purdue
because of his loyalty to the state of Indiana — the residents
of that state put a lot of pressure on him to stay at home —
and because of his desire to stay close to his family. Plus,
Purdue sweetened the deal by giving George's favorite
receiver in 1984 and favorite receiver in 1985 scholarships
even though both players weren't Division I caliber.

Before George signed with Purdue, the George family and then-coach Leon Burtnett met with Purdue's athletic director and president. The school administrators promised the Georges and Burtnett that Burtnett would be Purdue's coach throughout George's career. It's quite common for high-profile recruits in football and men's basketball to seek and get that type of assurance.

Purdue lied.

Halfway through George's freshman year, Purdue announced that Burtnett would be fired at the end of the year. The Georges were worried. Purdue administrators eased their fears by promising to hire a head coach with experience working with a pro-style quarterback.

Purdue lied.

The Boilermakers hired Fred Akers, the former Texas coach who made a name for himself by instructing quarterbacks to hand off to Earl Campbell.

With millions of dollars riding on his college development and feeling betrayed by the Purdue administration, George announced he was transferring. He wanted to stay in the Big Ten and close to home, but Big Ten rules prevented an in-conference transfer from receiving an athletic scholarship. So George orally committed to Miami. He never enrolled. The Hurricanes signed a hot-shot quarterback recruit by the name of Craig Erickson and lost interest in George.

George's parents paid his way, and he enrolled at Illinois and stayed three seasons — two playing and one sitting out as a transfer. There were no problems. In fact, he led the Illini to a 10-2 record (the most victories in one season in school history) and compiled some amazing fourth-quarter passing statistics.

After four years of college football, and with one year of remaining eligibility, George declared for the NFL draft after it became apparent he had a good chance of being the No. 1 pick. With the kind of money paid to No. 1-drafted quarterbacks, it made sense for George to leave Illinois.

What didn't make good football sense was George's desire to play for the Colts. George and his agent, Leigh Steinberg, engineered a scenario in which the Falcons traded the No. 1 pick to George's hometown team, the Colts. Again, George was the innocent victim of his naive loyalty to his hometown, home state, family and friends. While George was dreaming of leading his hometown team to the Super Bowl, he did not stop to consider that at the time the Colts were the worst-run franchise in professional sports. The Colts were run by Jim Irsay, the owner's son. Irsay had zero qualifications for the job. If you don't believe me, ask Carl Peterson or anyone who knows anything about pro football.

Over the next four years, George, the high-priced, home-town hero, became the scapegoat and the whipping boy for the Colts' institutionalized stupidity. The local news media, partially out of cowardice and partially because George's mannerisms are easily misconstrued as cocky and arrogant, never pointed a finger of blame at Irsay's incompetence.

George, like all of his teammates, grew frustrated with the team's mismanagement, and he also felt betrayed by his hometown. He reacted immaturely. He tried to force a trade by sitting out training camp in 1993.

In 1994, Colts owner Bob Irsay finally realized that his son was overmatched running a football team, so he hired Bill Tobin to run the team. Tobin prefers a ground-dominated offense and didn't want to spend time patching up a messy relationship, so he traded George to the Falcons.

In his rush to leave Indianapolis and because of his naiveté, George never stopped to consider that Tobin's hiring in Indianapolis made the Falcons the worst-run franchise in pro football. If you don't believe me, ask Peterson or any-one who knows anything about pro football.

So George, the quarterback who left Indianapolis wanting to prove to everyone that he's a winner, landed in the lap of a hopeless loser. The 2 1/2 years in Atlanta have been frustration-filled for George. The Falcons have an awful defense and rely on an offensive scheme — the run-and-punt — that everyone else in the league long ago decided was a joke.

Throughout it all, though, George and Coach June Jones maintained a close relationship. This season was vitally important to George's career. If he played well, he would either sign a long-term, big-money contract with the Falcons or become a valuable unrestricted free agent at the end of the year.

On national television, after completing 10 consecutive passes, George threw an interception on a pass on which a defensive lineman viciously hit him just as he released the ball. Jones benched him.

On the sideline, George yelled, "Are you going to give up on your quarterback three games into the season?" That started a heated shouting match between George and Jones. It reminded me of Bill Parcells and Phil Simms. No way should it have led to a suspension.

For shouting at a coach — something that happens routinely in the NFL — George may be forced to sit out longer than Irvin had to for having a cocaine-and-marijuana fiesta with a couple of self-employed models.

"I'm sorry for what I did," George said Wednesday. "I made a mistake. I'm a competitor, and I didn't want to give up. I thought I gave our team the best chance to win."

As for why he nixed a trade to Seattle just before Tuesday's trade deadline?

"I've made some mistakes, some bad decisions over the last seven years," said George, 28. "I don't want to rush into this decision. I want this to be a career decision. I want this to be the last team I play for. I want to make the right choice, and that will take time."

Peterson and the Chiefs need to spend some time getting to know the truth about Jeff George. This talented quarterback is likely to be available on the waiver wire in the next two weeks and then, because of his contract, probably will go unclaimed and be up for grabs. His No. 1 concern right now is winning, not money. The experiences in Indianapolis and Atlanta have humbled and matured him. He's a Midwesterner who would embrace this city, the people and our food.

And if given an opportunity to contribute to a Super Bowl-caliber team, he would reward Peterson, Marty Schottenheimer, Lamar Hunt and Chiefs fans with complete loyalty.

My life as a Playboy mole
January 30, 2003

There are a lot of great perks to being a somewhat famous sports writer. Partying with Hugh Hefner is at the top of the list.

Now I know how John Elway must've felt the first time he gripped an inflated pigskin, the elation that overcame Richard Petty when he first pressed pedal to metal, the sense of self-importance that engulfed Keyshawn Johnson after his first interview, and the rush of adrenaline (and blood) that energized Ron Jeremy the first time he heard a director shout "Take 2!"

You can waste your entire life searching for your calling, jumping from job to job, bad relationship to bad relationship, religion to religion.

Luckily, I discovered my life's calling Saturday night. Last week, I shared with you my angst about whether I should attend Hugh Hefner's Super Bowl soiree at San Diego's House of Hospitality in Balboa Park. The party was scheduled the night before The Big Game, which meant I wouldn't get to do my normal game preparation with some of the most respected names in football journalism. Also, I shared with you that over the years I had grown arousingly more uncomfortable with the NFL's association with beer advertisements that rely on the sexual objectification of intelligent women. And I admitted that I was enraged by a Budweiser commercial that insinuated that men with "cute little hands" had shortcomings.

As a man with "cute little hands," I feel the beer ads are now hitting below the belt, and it's time for commissioner Tagliabue and the league to stand against such negative, dehumanizing, dangerous stereotypes. The chains that bind sports to sex, athletes to supermodels, competition to decadence, beer to babes, and, dare I say, hand to ... well, you know ... must be broken.

So, as a man of principle, I considered declining my invitation to Hef's Playboy bash.

But hundreds of you reached out to me via e-mail and insisted that I attend the party. You said it was important as a journalist that I visit the front lines of the sports-sex-ploitation industry and report back to you the untold atrocities. You referenced the great men and women of history who made countless sacrifices for the betterment of mankind, and said that attending Hef's party was my opportunity to give back, to honor the old men of my profession, the Edwin Popes, the Furman Bishers, the Ralph Wileys.

Plus, my father called from his favorite barstool at the Masterpiece Lounge: "Negro, is you crazy? You go and represent. And you better take plenty pictures. Just be careful 'round all those sweet-smellin' Missy Annes. BellBiv-Devoe said it right. 'Never trust a big butt and a smile.' I don't know 'bout your generation. Every time you get a little money and fame ..."

Not wanting to let all of you down, I decided to attend the party. I'm glad I did. Researching the relationship between sports and scantily-clad, gorgeous women, I believe, is my calling. It's what I was put on this earth to do.

In order to rid professional sports leagues of their reliance on sexual exploitation, someone has to work from the inside, someone has to document the horrors, someone has to hang out with the biggest stars in sports and listen to their gossip, and someone has to befriend the half-naked models and try to convince them that being the girlfriend of a sportswriter has more perks than being a one-night stand of an NFL star.

This is my calling. It has to be. It came so natural to me.

My first good decision was ignoring the overwhelming sentiment expressed by readers of this column who told me to attend the party stag. A Hef party is the one shindig in which it is perfectly acceptable and beneficial to bring sand to the beach. Plus, I needed someone to take pictures.

Finding a date to a Hef party, even a thousand miles away

from home, is about as easy as finding a roll on Warren Sapp's neck. Dangling an invite to the Playboy party all week had women calling me Denzel Whitlockton by Friday night. I'm not so sure it made me all that popular with my sportswriting peers. Randy Covitz, my colleague from Kansas City, threw me under a bus when he overheard me sweet-talking the NFL's most beautiful public-relations staffer, Morgan.

"Hey, Jason, I thought you had some girl from Kansas City coming out here to stay with you," Covitz blurted out in the middle of my conversation with Morgan.

Hate the game, Randy, not the playa.

So I ended up taking Amy, a friend who works as a hotel front-desk clerk in San Diego and snagged a temporary media credential by pretending to be a producer for a radio show. She's smart, adventurous and cute, the perfect combination for a Hef party.

I decided to go with a dressy, casual look. I wore a dark blue, sleeveless suit, you know, the kind Cedric the Entertainer wore on the Kings of Comedy Tour. To make it casual, I went without a tie and wore a navy silk shirt, untucked.

"You look important, but like you came to have a good time," Amy said.

The party started at 9:30 p.m. We arrived at 8:30. Hey, the invite said we needed to check in by 8:45. As we stood around waiting to be let in, we got the chance to observe several party-crashers try to talk their way in. Victoria, the lady with the VIP, ticketless guests list, was tough. She wasn't falling for any B.S.

The House of Hospitality is really just a gigantic, luxurious visitors' center for Balboa Park. As you walked into Hef's party, there was a huge open courtyard. Patriots quarterback Tom Brady was the first celeb that I spotted. He was holding court in the courtyard with a couple of female fans.

Straight ahead a giant ballroom had been turned into a hip-hop dance club. Marcus Allen, fresh from his election into the Pro Football Hall of Fame, was back in the ballroom, celebrating with Ronnie Lott and Vencie Glenn. Warren Moon hung out by the exit.

To the right of the courtyard was the Prado restaurant, which has nice outdoor patio dining. I ran into Shannon Sharpe and Tony Gonzalez inside the restaurant. Gonzalez tried to introduce me to Carmen Electra, but she insisted that we talk in the VIP area. I didn't have a VIP pass. Gonzalez and Sharpe followed Carmen into the VIP area, and I never saw them again. Outside, I talked to Tony Siragusa, John Rocker, John Salley and Barry Sanders.

I know what you're thinking. Forget about the athletes. What about the girls?

Trust me, I was thinking the same thing. Hef had the place stuffed with beautiful women. But besides a few women dressed in only well-placed body paint and G-strings, the party wasn't all that decadent. It wasn't even rated R.

Yeah, I met the Miller Lite catfight girls, got a kiss from one of Hef's bunnies, a drunken woman sat on my lap and whispered what she would be willing to do to me if I'd introduce her to Hef. (Hugh, you can reach me at 816-234-4869.)

But beyond that, I was disappointed. What I learned is that these parties are really for the big, big stars. Sharpe and Gonzalez had women all over them. Kordell Stewart rapped with the finest, thickest woman at the party. Women threw themselves at Barry Sanders.

A woman spotted me talking to Warren Moon and came up and introduced herself. Amaya was her name. Nice girl. I was right in the middle of asking for her cellphone number when Warren walked away.

"You're not with Warren?" she asked.

"No," I said.

She walked away.

Becoming a real insider in the sports-sexual-exploitation

world might take years and years of dedication. For you, I will take on this challenge, this burden. It is my calling.

■

Situation establishes credentials
January 15, 1995

Jason is one of the few sports columnists in the country who routinely uses his real-life experiences and real-life friends to make a strong point about what's going on in the sports world. As the NCAA enacted the Proposition 16 eligibility standards Jason talked about a college friend who was a Proposition 48 qualifier.

One of my best friends is a guy named Keith Stalling. At the same time I played football at Ball State, he played basketball there.

The D.O.C., that's what we call Keith, grew up in the Englewood Community of Chicago. Englewood isn't nearly as infamous as Compton, Calif., but it's twice as dangerous and more impoverished.

In 1987, with one trash bag of clothes, and a Proposition-48 label, the D.O.C. took a bus to Ball State. Five years later, he left with a business degree and the respect of everyone who came in contact with him.

Whenever the NCAA discusses academic standards, as it did last week in San Diego, I think about the D.O.C. and about how common sense needs to be added to America's debate over qualifications.

Last week the NCAA reaffirmed its decision to toughen academic entrance requirements for student-athletes, ratifying Proposition 16, a tougher version of the already-implemented Prop 48.

Beginning in 1996, incoming freshmen will face a sliding-academic scale for athletic eligibility. Since 1986, freshmen basically have needed a 2.0 grade-point average and a 700 SAT score or a 17 ACT score to be eligible for an athletic scholarship and to play as a freshman.

Next year, the SAT and ACT requirements will escalate depending on GPA. A 2.0 GPA means an athlete will need a 900 SAT or 21 ACT. The old SAT and ACT scores will be OK if an athlete has a 2.5 GPA.

The Black Coaches Association, most notably its high-profile men's basketball coaches, has threatened mass protest if Prop 16 is enacted. The BCA has stressed that relying on standardized tests will affect black athletes disproportionately.

The NCAA, which could be accurately described as the WPA (White Presidents Association), is determined to improve its image. The NCAA has bought into the popular-but-simple-minded Newt World Order, meaning it plans to meet its goal by telling a slice of the population that it's unqualified.

Both parties — the BCA and the NCAA — are in error.

The BCA never should have allowed the debate to be over race. And, if the NCAA truly is interested in academic performance, it should focus on what athletes do once they're on campus rather than what they did before enrollment.

But today we're discussing qualifications. The NCAA only needs to add common sense to the GPA standardized-test equation. By adding common sense we would realize that class (i.e., economic standing), not race, is at the crux of the debate, and we would abhor the idea of hindering athletes such as the D.O.C. from attending college.

The D.O.C. and I are both black. Without a minute of preparation, I scored an 880 on the SAT. Despite coaching and three attempts, the D.O.C. never scored higher than 11 on the ACT.

The D.O.C. rode two buses and one train on his hour-long trek to Dunbar High, a school that specializes in training electricians and mechanics. I drove the car my mother gave me exactly one mile to Warren Central High, one of the best-funded schools in Indianapolis.

The D.O.C. spent his entire school day looking over his back. His school was overrun by warring gangs. I spent most of my school day wondering what was on the lunch menu.

There are countless other differences and there are numerous studies showing a link between parental income and success on the SAT and ACT, but I'm going to stop and simply say:

There would be no debate between the BCA and the WPA, er, NCAA if we determined qualifications fairly in this country.

■

Wiley's Royko-like qualities made him my hero
June 15, 2004

Jason found out about the death of his idol, Ralph Wiley, while vacationing in Germany. How many people get to become dear friends with their childhood idol? Ralph saw himself in Jason. And Jason saw who he wanted to be in Ralph.

FRANKFURT, Germany - It's a strange twist that the two men who most heavily influenced my journalistic career both died well before their time and had such divergent backgrounds.

Mike Royko and Ralph Wiley, as far as I know, had little in common, sans my unabashed passion for their work. Royko was an angry and hilarious, old, white Chicago newspaper columnist and Pulitzer Prize winner. His plain-spoken and opinionated, nationally syndicated column captured my imagination as a child.

Wiley was an angry and provocative black writer for Sports Illustrated and an author of several books. Wiley first came to my attention when I was a teenager and he made an appearance on Phil Donahue's show. Wiley embarrassed a member of the Ku Klux Klan with his quick wit and dismissive attitude. I became an instant fan and began to follow his work in magazines and on television.

Shortly after suffering a brain aneurysm, Royko died in
1997 at the age of 64. At the time of his death, his column
was still the best thing about the newspaper industry.
Wiley, 52, died Sunday night after suffering heart failure
while watching the NBA finals. His work for ESPN.com
was one of the best things about the Internet.

I never met Mike Royko. I wrote him several times at the
Chicago Tribune. I always received a form letter in return.
I was never offended. Royko had hundreds of thousands
of fans, and he was an extremely busy man. Just before
Royko passed, a local organization here got one of
Royko's assistants to send me a framed photo of Royko.
The picture hangs in my home office.

I have many vivid memories of Ralph Wiley. We became
dear friends over the last six or seven years. I can't even
recall how we met. I do remember my first words to
Ralph: "You're my idol. You and Mike Royko are why
I'm in this business."

I loved Mike Royko because he was fearless, outspoken,
agenda free and funny. I loved Ralph Wiley because he
was my symbol that a black man could be fearless, outspoken, uncompromised and successful in America.

I wanted to be like Mike, and Ralph's success said I could

be a black version of Mike Royko if that's what my heart desired.

My life the past 10 years in Kansas City in many ways has been like a fantasy, and my dear friend Ralph Wiley is partially responsible. He paved the way for black sportswriters. During his nine years at SI, he fought the political battles at the magazine and excelled even though he felt a glass ceiling was trying to hinder his success. Ralph was one of the first sportswriters to make regular appearances on one of the NFL's pre-game shows. He worked for NBC. He was one of the first black sportswriters to appear on ESPN's Sports Reporters show. He performed a weekly commentary for "SportsCenter."

Ralph wrote books with Spike Lee and Dexter Scott King, Martin Luther King Jr.'s son. Most recently, Ralph had served as one of the anchor columnists for ESPN.com's wildly popular Page 2. His column had a unique style and flair — he intentionally took indirect routes to make his point — and a rabid following. He was controversial, mysterious and unpredictable.

His body of work in print and broadcast clearly establishes him as one of the best sports journalists of our time. As a friend, he was even better than that.

Despite a ridiculous schedule, Ralph always had time whenever I called looking for advice or looking to gossip.

A little more than a week ago, Ralph stopped in Kansas City to meet with his son, Cole, and his niece, Kim. Ralph's niece lives here and his son, a recent college graduate, was passing through here on his way to California. We all met and had dinner at Garozzo's. Ralph liked visiting Kansas City. He loved the Negro Leagues Baseball Museum. He planned on talking Spike Lee into doing a documentary on the museum and a player.

Ralph seemed to be in good health. We argued and laughed at dinner for two hours. Ralph was excited. He had several major projects in the works for ESPN. He wasn't done making an impact on this business. He was ready to reach new heights.

The next day, Ralph and Cole crammed into Cole's car and began driving toward California.

"It was perfect, it was meant to be," Ralph's fiancee, Susan Peacock, told me Monday night from the Florida home she and Ralph shared. "Ralph got to spend that father-son time with Cole that he so enjoyed. Cole was everything to him."

Ralph flew back to Florida after helping Cole settle in California. Sunday night, long after a passionate appearance on an ESPN radio program and just moments after player introductions during the NBA finals, Ralph doubled over in pain and died.

" 'It's up to you all in the younger generation to carry on' is what Ralph would say," Susan Peacock shared.

It's an honor to carry on in Ralph's memory.

Ralph Wiley, 1952-2004

One of the original Page 2 columnists at ESPN.com, he wrote more than 240 columns between November 2000 and June 2004. Hired by Sports Illustrated in 1982, he remained there nine years, writing 28 cover stories, mostly about boxing. He also wrote three books and co-authored several more.

*Jason and Trent Green
at the Playboy Super
Bowl party.*

*At one of Jason's holiday parties Carl Peterson tells
Whitlock Claus what he wants for Christmas; Abe Lincoln
separates the two and keeps the peace.*

*At Hugh Hefner's Super
Bowl Party Jason takes
a break from his inves-
tigative responsibilities
to pose for a picture
with Marcus Allen.*

Following an unfortunate event in New England during a Patriots-Chiefs game, Jason found himself in need of a little legal guidance...

Jason and Ollie Gates (far left) want to talk barbeque, but Carol Coe and Mayor Pro-Tem Alvin Brooks keep bringing up politics.

At the Playboy Super Bowl Party Shannon Sharpe (left) and Tony Gonzalez (right) take time to thank the man who showed them how to play tight end.

Roy Williams sits down to chat with Jason at the annual Christmas party; even after the painful departure to North Carolina Williams remains Jason's favorite coach. In the middle, Steven "MU Rock" St. John tries not to nod off.

Jason and his father hold court at his dad's bar, the world famous Masterpiece Lounge in Indianapolis.

In 1997 Jeff George finally came to Arrowhead, but he was wearing the wrong jersey. The weekend of the Raiders visit Jason and his favorite linebacker (Derrick Thomas, right) took some barbeque down to his favorite quarterback (Jeff George, left).

Starting the Turkey Bowl is one of Jason's proudest accomplishments during his time in Kansas City. Jason and Union Broadcasting President Chad Boeger (next to Jason) launched the event as a fundraiser for Harvesters and the annual game is now one of the city's best-known charity events.

Jason and his mom in the kitchen; Jason insists that no one has yet topped his mother's cooking, but sources say Johnson County Soccer Mom Champion Susie May (behind Jason) has put together a solid challenge.

At his annual holiday party Jason takes a moment to get a picture with Tony Temple, his favorite high school athlete.

Chapter 2

This Is Going to Hurt Me More than It's Going to Hurt You: Sometimes You Have to Come Down Hard

What Texas wants,
KC must keep
March 9, 1997

Responding to Jason's column on the first Big 12 Tournament (chapter 4) Texas Longhorns' coach Tom Penders took the bait and fired some shots back. The Texas schools then put on an embarrassing display and were all on their way home by Friday. Jason penned this column as the last of the Texas teams left Kansas City.

Someone stop that orange Southwest Airlines flying bus, the one with Texas coach Tom Penders and his band of underachievers on it.

I've got something I'd like to say to Penders, the coach who should be headed to the NIT, the coach who has never had a whiff of the Final Four, the basketball genius who got slapped around by Norm Stewart and a bunch of Tigers that only won 13 regular-season games.

Tom, before you threaten to move the Big 12 men's basketball tournament to another city, win a game first, gain some clout, do something besides getting recognized as a decent basketball coach in a now-defunct, corrupt football league.

Tom, believe it or not, this is Roy's and Norm's and

Eddie's and Tim's and Kelvin's conference. You've got some major dues to pay before anyone outside of Austin, Texas, cares what you have to say.

Come talk to us after you make the NIT final four, Tom.

Ladies and gentlemen of Kansas City, Penders is a perfect example of the kind of Texas arrogance that could cost us the Big 12 tournament.

Penders' resume has more holes in it than O.J's alibi. But after one day and one defeat in Kansas City, Tommy feels qualified to threaten power-brokering the tournament's removal from Kansas City.

"I don't want to pass judgment," Penders said shortly after Missouri bounced the second-seeded Longhorns on Friday, "but if we're not going to be treated as part of the league, then there's a good chance this tournament might be moved around a little bit."

What sparked Penders' asinine remark?

My little, tongue-in-cheek column in Thursday's Star that lampooned the state of Texas' suspect college basketball history and the state's stereotypical down-home ways.

The column was a joke, playing off the tension between the Big 12's North and South divisions. There was nothing all that unusual about the shtick. Popular Dallas sports columnist Randy Galloway regularly rips into Arkansas Razorback fans, and Denver's top sports columnist, Woody Paige, annually belittles Nebraska Cornvicts faithful.

Penders may not be much of a basketball coach, but his travels have certainly made him worldly. He's trying to covertly use my column as an excuse to vent his (and other Texans') true feelings about the future of the Big 12 tournament.

He wants it out of Kansas City. As soon as possible.

My feel from spending the weekend hanging around Kemper Arena is that so do a lot of other Texans. If you listen to the Big 12 power people closely enough, you can hear them quietly crafting in their minds the excuses and rationalizations they need to justify moving the tournament to Texas after the year 2000.

"We want to keep the women's and men's tournaments together," they say. "The women would draw better crowds in Texas."

And, of course, as Dallas Morning News columnist Kevin Blackistone pointed out quite eloquently to his Texas readers on Friday and to Kansas Citians on Saturday, there's our "Blunder Down Under" or "Dump with a Hump," breathtaking Kemper Arena.

Texans are going to try to use Kemper as an excuse to move the tournament. And, quite frankly, it's a legitimate complaint. Our visionaries over at the Greater Kansas City Sports Commission talked us into wasting $20 million to give our livestock warehouse a face-lift. No matter what our chamber-of-commerce, let's-make-everyone-comfortable TV news reporters tell you, the renovation was a waste. The visionaries who supported this move need to be held accountable.

We need a new arena. Period.

And we also need to change the way we deal with Texans. It's time we get off our knees, unpucker our lips, look these people in the eye and tell them they're dealing with their equal. We tried begging and fanny-kissing, and they took the conference office anyway.

In his column, Blackistone suggested that Big 12 commissioner Steve Hatchell did us a favor by leaving the tournament here. That is typical Texas thinking.

As if playing host to the Big Eight tournament in a first-class manner for 20 straight years didn't earn us the right.

Texans aren't bad people. They aren't ignorant. Their women know how to dress. But the fact is Texans have never looked at anything, no matter how successful, without thinking, "You know, we could do that better in Texas, knowwhatImean?"

Well, we don't know.

The Texas schools won one game in this tournament, and Texas Tech, the school that brought us Byron Hanspard and the 0.00 grade-point average, had to forfeit that victory after the Red Raiders admitted at halftime of their second game that they were using two academically ineligible players.

Unfortunately, that is typical Texas, too. Texans cheated the Southwest Conference into extinction. Supporters of the old Big Eight should be reluctant to turn over all of the Big 12's jewels to folks who have yet to learn their lesson.

■

Councilwoman misplaces race
in arena debate
July 25, 2004

In the summer of 2004 Kansas City prepared for an August vote that included a tax on rental cars and hotel rooms to help finance a new arena in downtown. Mayor Kay Barnes had already secured millions in private financing and was hoping to raise the rest through her new tourism tax proposal. Enterprise Rent-a-Car of St. Louis was the loudest voice of opposition but certain local figures also spoke out against the plan. Since this column appeared numerous figures in the black community have condemned Jason for making these comments about a black politician.

The arguments against Mayor Kay Barnes' plan to finance a downtown arena hit a new low last week when Kansas City Councilwoman Saundra McFadden-Weaver decided to enter the discussion.

McFadden-Weaver, sensing an opportunity to make a complete clown of herself and steal some of the spotlight from the Enterprise Rent-A-Car meddlers, out-Bozo-ed Ringling Brothers by interjecting race into the debate.

"How about the fact that 40 percent of the largest rental car service cars are rented by the African-American population or minorities of Kansas City?" she stated at a news conference on Monday. "Something about this deal does not celebrate diversity."

McFadden-Weaver was referring to the up to $4 per day rental-car fee Mayor Barnes wants voters to approve. Fees placed on hotels and car rentals will help finance the new arena, if Mayor Barnes' proposal is passed on Aug. 3. Barnes' plan makes sense. But Enterprise Rent-A-Car, a St. Louis-based company, is spending close to $500,000 trying to defeat Barnes' proposal. (Editor's note: the final amount was about twice this much)

Political clowns such as McFadden-Weaver are using Mayor Barnes' arena package as a means to play politics and draw attention to themselves.

Today, let's give McFadden-Weaver the attention she so desperately wants. She said during a radio interview Friday that black people will be disproportionately affected by Mayor Barnes' financing proposal.

"And I do see means by which we'll be disproportionately affected," freedom-fighter McFadden-Weaver babbled, "because we live in the urban core, where when you look at car rental taxes, then the largest company of car rental is strategically located in our area."

Say what? Most cars are rented at the airport. I wouldn't

exactly say our airport is located in the "urban core."

"My point is that local citizens of Kansas City may be un-awarely taxed by this," McFadden-Weaver further explained during her radio interview, "and so we're questioning as to whether or not it really is a tax that will come from our tourists and whether or not we're going to have an increase in income (tax). As you know in Kansas City, if you're under that economic radar called poverty, if you're in the poverty area or if you're poorer, the question would be whether or not you would ever afford a ticket in that arena unless you're given a job in the arena."

As you know, if you've spent any time in Kansas City and have followed Rev. McFadden-Weaver's career, she's unqualified for political office and is doing her district more harm than good. She thinks she's a savvy negotiator. She thinks if she creates a big enough stink by throwing around substance-less, racial Molotov Cocktails, she'll get something in return.

"I'm excited about it," McFadden-Weaver said of the arena project. "I think it will be a great project. And I think it should generate a great, great amount of jobs. We've just not been given that in writing and we're waiting to get it. I'm scheduled for a meeting (Saturday) with the mayor and city manager (Wayne Cauthen). ... I'm sure that when the mayor and city manager and I sit down that we're going to come to a very favorable agreement that will affect the citizens and taxpayers of Kansas City."

I hope someone told McFadden-Weaver to shut up. She's made her district look foolish. She's undermined her own ability to tackle legitimate racial issues, of which there are plenty in Kansas City. She has unfairly and recklessly called into question Mayor Barnes' integrity and the integrity of her proposal.

And for what purpose? And on what grounds?

When McFadden-Rosa-Parks-Weaver was asked by her radio interviewer where her statistics about car-rental tendencies came from, she reached for her big red nose, purple wig and huge floppy shoes.

"That number to my understanding comes from the general averages from across the country," McFadden-Weaver replied, "and we had no reason to think that Kansas City was outside the norm. But, as I said earlier, my urban economist is researching that for me and will get that to me this evening."

McFadden-Weaver employs an "urban economist?" Does everyone on the Kansas City council get an "urban" or "suburban" economist based on their preference?

Is it too late to put McFadden-Weaver's ouster on the Aug. 3 ballot? The 3rd district deserves far better representation than McFadden-Weaver. According to my "urban pollster," 100 percent of her constituency is being misrepresented.

Something about McFadden-Weaver's statement regarding Mayor Barnes' arena proposal does not celebrate sanity.

■

Faith in Robinson dooms KC
January 12, 2004

During his time in Kansas City Jason has done his best to rip apart some coaches. Few have suffered attacks as harsh as the ones he threw on former Chiefs' defensive coordinator Greg Robinson. In 2002 Kansas City allowed more yards than any other defense and in 2003 they ranked 29th. Following the playoff debacle against the Colts where the Chiefs failed to force a single Indianapolis punt Jason laid the blame for failure squarely on Robinson.

The loyalty that doomed Kansas City's 2003 football season before it even began reared its heartbreaking head one last time Sunday inside Arrowhead Stadium, host of the Chiefs' playoff showdown against the Indianapolis Colts.

As the Chiefs were rallying and trying to keep pace with Indianapolis' unstoppable offense, Dick Vermeil placed one last bit of faith in Greg Robinson's defense. Having sliced Indy's lead to seven points with 4 minutes, 22 seconds to play, Vermeil instructed kicker Jason Baker to fake an onside kick and boot the ball deep.

Vermeil asked Robinson's unit to do what it had been unable to do all day — stop Peyton Manning and Indianapolis' offense from scoring. Vermeil might as well have asked Pete Rose to tell the truth.

"You never know," Vermeil explained when asked why he thought Kansas City's defense could stop Manning. "I just did what I thought was right at the time."

Last off-season, Vermeil thought the right thing to do was bring back the coordinator of the NFL's worst defense. Vermeil convinced himself that all it would take to fix Robinson's 32nd-ranked defense was a few free-agent acquisitions and the return of a couple of injured veterans.

The stupidity of that belief was evident Sunday as the Colts expelled from the playoffs yet another 13-3 Chiefs squad blessed with the backing of a rabid sellout crowd and a bye week of rest.

Colts 38, Chiefs 31.

Kansas City failed to advance for a multitude of reasons, but primarily because Robinson's unit didn't force a punt or turnover or provide KC's offense and special teams any margin for error. Only the halftime-whistle stopped Indianapolis' offense from scoring. At the end of the game, the Chiefs got the ball back with 8 seconds on the clock. The Colts turned down a makable field-goal attempt and went for it on fourth and 3 from the KC 28.

"We faced a really, really good offense," Robinson said. "We gave 'em everything we had."

If that's the truth, the Chiefs don't have much. The faith and loyalty Dick Vermeil showed Greg Robinson last off-season and with a little more than 4 minutes left in this season were totally inappropriate.

"Even as a defensive player, after 55 minutes of not being able to stop them and being so frustrated, yeah, maybe we should've gone for the (onside kick)," defensive end Vonnie Holliday acknowledged.

"The percentages aren't good," Vermeil said of an onside kick.

There was a better chance of the Chiefs recovering an onside kick than stopping Manning, who expertly directed Indy's offense. Manning threw for 304 yards and three TDs, running his offense from the line of scrimmage as usual despite a deafening crowd at Arrowhead Stadium. Vermeil, Robinson and Kansas City's players showered praise on Manning.

"All day, one guy was one step ahead of us," Holliday said.

"It would be unfair to not give (Manning) the credit he deserves," Robinson said.

Manning was brilliant. But we're not talking about a Wilt Chamberlain-esque one-man scoring machine. This wasn't Michael Jordan raining three-pointers on the Portland Trail Blazers. Yes, Manning was in a zone. A pass-rush-free zone. He was playing seven on seven. The Chiefs never hurried him. Because he consistently brought Indy's offense to the line of scrimmage with 20 seconds on the play clock, Manning had plenty of time to read Robinson's poorly disguised blitzes and coverages.

I could read them from the press box, and I haven't been in an offensive meeting room in more than a decade. Seriously, KC's corners weren't hard to read. Every time they faked a corner blitz and fell back into a zone, Manning would hit Marvin Harrison or Reggie Wayne matched up against safeties Greg Wesley or Jerome Woods. You could see it coming within two or three steps of Harrison getting off the line. My colleague Ivan Carter called out Wayne's 19-yard, third-quarter TD before the snap. Carter saw what Manning saw: Dexter McCleon matched up one-on-one just after being burned on consecutive slant patterns by Wayne. It's embarrassing that one motivated and liberated young quarterback can outthink an entire defensive coaching staff.

You can't explain away Indianapolis' 38 points and no punts by saying that Manning had a once-in-a-lifetime performance. Robinson's defensive scheme is just as responsible. He can't be retained. KC's fan base has had enough of Robinson, and so have the Chiefs' defensive players. Vermeil needs to show Robinson the same amount of loyalty he shows a non-productive player in training camp.

Will Vermeil be too loyal?

"You're gonna have to address that with Dick Vermeil," said Chiefs president Carl Peterson, who leaves coaching-staff decisions to his head coach. "Dick will make the right decision."

I'd like to believe that. But when it comes to issues involving loyalty, Vermeil can convince himself of almost anything. He actually believed Robinson's outfit played significantly better inside Arrowhead Stadium. He actually believed Robinson's unit had a shot at stopping Manning late in the game.

It would be funny if these 13-3 losses didn't hurt so much.

■

Kansas doesn't need 'Shallow Al'
February 13, 2003

Al Bohl will forever be remembered as the man who ran off Roy Williams. The former Fresno State athletic director came to KU to help rebuild the football program, but he'll be best remembered as the kook who said Roy crushed him like a dove. A month before rumors of Williams' departure to Carolina started, Jason offered this harsh assessment of Bohl and foreshadowed Roy's departure.

In Al Bohl's world, wherever that is, he probably does have a wonderful relationship with Roy Williams and Mark Mangino and everyone else in the Kansas athletic department.

Al Bohl's world is a happy place where everyone paints on a phony smile, makes nice talk and is tickled pink that the Kansas athletic director always has something clever and upbeat to say.

The problem for Al Bohl is that he's the lone inhabitant of his planet. Everyone else lives in reality.

Al Bohl probably thinks I like him. Every time our paths cross at a Kansas athletic event, I put a big smile on my face, shake his hand and laugh out loud at whatever comes out of his mouth. I rarely know what he says. I just know

I'm supposed to laugh because he laughs first. If you've met Al Bohl, you know exactly what I'm talking about. An encounter with Bohl is uncomfortable. Not because he's menacing or dangerous or conniving. It's uncomfortable

Al Bohl speaks to the media in front of his house in Lawrence after he was fired as athletic director at KU. It was this interview where Bohl made his famous "...crushed like a dove" statement.

because it always feels unnatural and phony. No matter how many times you meet Al Bohl, it always feels like the first time. There's no depth.

That's why it's not surprising that Shallow Al had to spend the better part of Wednesday afternoon defending himself and combating rumors that he's on the verge of being fired and doesn't get along with KU's most influential coaches, Williams and Mangino.

Robert Hemenway, KU's chancellor, issued a vote of confidence in support of Bohl.

Big mistake.

Bohl needs to be fired. He was brought to Kansas because he allegedly had expertise in two areas, picking a football coach and fund-raising. We've come to learn that Bohl really has expertise in only one. Fresno State is still cleaning up the mess Shallow Al created in its athletic department when he conveniently transferred reserve funds to balance the budget.

So Bohl has pretty much done all he can do at Kansas. He tabbed Mangino to resurrect Kansas' moribund football program. I tend to doubt that Mangino needs Bohl as a wingman as he tries to battle Bill Snyder's monster.

Nope. Mangino needs a credible fund-raiser. The Kansas athletic department needs a credible fund-raiser. And, more important, the university needs an athletic director who gets along with the university's highest-profile employee, Roy Williams.

Rumors about a strain in Bohl's relationship with Williams have circulated ever since Bohl fired football coach Terry Allen, Williams' good friend, with three games left in the 2001 season. Williams didn't like it and made his dislike of Bohl's action public knowledge.

Bohl never rebounded. He mishandled Williams. Instead of making peace with his No. 1 employee, Bohl made comments stating that Williams needed to realize Bohl was the CEO of the athletic department. Big mistake. You don't strong-arm an institution, particularly one that generates lots of revenue and had 20,000 supporters come out to a football stadium to hear him say "I'm stayin'."

Hey, I can't say unequivocally that Williams dislikes Bohl. Williams has done a decent job of putting on a public air of indifference when it comes to Shallow Al.

But if I were Williams, I wouldn't like Shallow Al. And it wouldn't have anything to do with Terry Allen. It would revolve around knowing that Oklahoma's Kelvin Sampson has Joe Castigilone, and Texas' Rick Barnes has DeLoss Dodds, and Missouri's Quin Snyder has Mike Alden making sure the Sooners, the Longhorns and the Tigers have everything they need to hunt down Williams' Jayhawks.

Roy's smart enough and humble enough to know that he can't keep his Jayhawks ahead of the rest of the Big 12 without the assistance of a wise A.D. Eventually, Kansas will pay a price for keeping Shallow Al around.

Quin needs to watch his back
December 12, 2003

Scandals are nothing new for the NCAA, but the Ricky Clemons saga at MU raised the level of embarrassment for athletic departments. Inappropriate payments, ATV accidents, going AWOL from detention centers, and taped phone conversations made this story worthy of a CIA style mystery movie...or maybe a daytime soap opera. Here Jason talks about what different parties had at stake after a series of poor decisions.

Quin Snyder be shakin' today.

His president, embattled, embarrassed and regretful University of Missouri systems president Elson Floyd, repeatedly distanced himself from Snyder and Snyder's under-NCAA-investigation basketball program Thursday afternoon at a news conference to address the Ricky Clemons-inspired jailhouse drama, "Ebonics, Lies and Audio Tape."

Asked whether he'd considered firing Snyder, Floyd, husband of relationship expert Carmento "Oprah X" Floyd, gave Snyder a chilly endorsement.

"That's a question that needs to be posed to the athletic director and not to me," Elson Floyd said. "Quin Snyder, with the work he's been engaged in with the basketball team, is continuing to perform for the university."

Asked specifically to assess how responsible Snyder is for the entire Clemons fiasco, Floyd covered just one (tail), and it wasn't Snyder's.

"Well, it's important for everyone in this room to know that I did not have anything to do with the recruiting or the admission of Ricky Clemons," Floyd said. "Ricky Clemons was here at the university when I arrived. So his entry into the university had nothing to do with me. In fact, I was in Michigan at the time."

Yeah, Quin be shakin'. Elson Floyd made it quite clear whom he blames for his wife's 1-800-collect relationship with TRicky Clemons. Floyd repeated that he and Carmento only got involved with TRicky because Snyder and the athletic department asked them to.

Which does or doesn't explain why Carmento and gal-pal Amy "Sista Soulja" Stewart, wife of associate athletic director Ed Stewart, were apparently rooting for the demise of the basketball program.

"I would have no way of knowing any of that," Elson Floyd said when asked about his wife's dislike of Mizzou's basketball program. "The truth of the matter is that..."

I interrupted Floyd and reminded him that it would be easy for him to ask his wife directly.

"You know," Floyd responded, "I did not talk to Carmento about any of these issues in part because I had advised her not to continue the engagement with Ricky."

At the start of the 2003-2004 season no coach in the country faced as much scrutiny as Quin Snyder. Here he is surrounded by reporters at Big 12 Media Day.

Okay. If Floyd told his wife to stop, why did she continue?

"There were several reasons for that," Elson Floyd said. "First of all, she has a very great nurturing part of her persona. So her mother instincts kicked in. As I said previously, she had worked at a facility that helped with the re-entry of individuals who had been incarcerated. And thirdly, there were serious injuries that had been sustained while he was at our residence. Those are the three reasons and those reasons alone."

That explanation I buy. The Floyds had a lot riding on TRicky's recovery. It was in their best interest to stay in TRicky's good graces.

It seems that Floyd believes he has little to gain by maintaining a warm-and-fuzzy relationship with Quin Snyder. But we better not read too much into Floyd's chilly feelings toward Snyder. Floyd's credibility has been damaged by his wife's racially-charged conversations with TRicky. Quin may have nothing to gain by maintaining a warm-and-fuzzy relationship with a lame-duck president.

What's painfully clear is that the Missouri athletic department and the administration are completely dysfunctional. But tough economic times may keep the Floyds, the Stewarts, the Snyders, the Aldens and Lil' TRicky all together in Columbia.

Before his news conference, Floyd addressed the board of curators and told them about Missouri's "fiscal crisis" and how that crisis would impact the entire school system in 2004. The University of Missouri just doesn't have the money at this time to buy out contracts or fight lawsuits.

In the words of Amy Stewart, they be stuck with each other.

■

It's plain to see: KC's King Carl wears no clothes
February 16, 1997

*During Jason's ten years in Kansas City there has been
one true constant throughout: Carl Peterson as general
manager, CEO, and president of the Chiefs. Jason and
Carl have at times had a rocky relationship, and Jason has
never hesitated to speak up about Peterson's flaws. In the
1997 off-season the Chiefs engaged in a brief, whirlwind
courtship with free agent quarterback Jeff George. George
voiced a strong preference to sign with the Chiefs, but
instead ended up with the Raiders. Jason examines what
happened, talks about the mistakes that cost Kansas City
George's laser arm, and, of course, never admits that
George was an NFL bust.*

Enlightening. That's the best word to describe my reaction to Carl Peterson's pathetic pursuit of quarterback Jeff
George, who officially became a Raider on Saturday.

Things that had been unclear about the Chiefs are now
coming into focus. Steve Bono, Lin Elliott, Trezelle
Jenkins and the Chiefs' love affair with washed-up, fading
quarterbacks make sense now.

Peterson was never really a king, only the benefactor of a
great tailor, a good voice and the ability to surround him-

self with brilliant men — Dick Vermeil, Marty Schottenheimer, Tim Connolly, Joe Montana and Marcus Allen.
The clothes, the voice and the men have conspired to
create an intoxicating aura for Peterson.

The George fiasco sobered me up.

Judging from Derrick Thomas' critical comments on
Thursday, some of the Chiefs' players are sobering up, too.
And judging by Schottenheimer's seizure of control over
draft decisions — yes, it happened — the Chiefs coaches
have sobered, as well.

Again, let me put us all on the same page. Yes, I thought it
would be good for George, my old high school teammate,
and the Chiefs if George played here. However, I never
thought the Chiefs should pay George the kind of money
Al Davis will. A KC deal only made sense if George was
willing to settle for a reasonable salary (five years, $20
million), which I believe he would have.

Also, had Peterson stated at the beginning that the Chiefs
were unwilling to pay George a reasonable salary, so therefore the Chiefs wouldn't pursue George, I would have
strongly disagreed with Peterson but would have respected
his right to hold such an opinion of a quarterback with such
a troubled past.

But that's not what Peterson did. With a straight face and

feeling it was a legitimate offer, he offered George $5.1 million over three years — less money than Bono was making.

He further damaged his credibility by committing a sin that no man in his 50s should commit. You never, never ever count another man's money. Never.

Sitting in Kansas City, Peterson tried to count Al Davis' money in Oakland. Peterson never believed — even as late as Friday — that the Raiders could come up with $27.5 million over five years.

"I still don't believe the deal is done," Peterson said around 3:45 p.m. Friday, hours after the ink had dried on George's contract.

I mention all this because it speaks to competence. How could a grown man reach the conclusion that another grown man with a family would take a job for more than $20 million less than his market value? How could a sup-posedly mature man make the mistake of trying to count another man's money? Is Peterson living in a fantasy world that tells him he's doing talented players a favor by letting them play for the Chiefs? How many Super Bowls does Peterson believe he has won?

Nearly two decades ago, Peterson hooked on to Vermeil's coattails and made it to a Super Bowl with the Eagles.

Thanks to Schottenheimer's coaching, the marketing wizardry of Connolly and the image-enhancing acquisitions of Montana and Allen, Peterson has been credited with creating a monster out at Arrowhead Stadium.

Now you've got to wonder whether we haven't all been buffaloed. Now those troubling questions we've put in the back of our minds must be dealt with.

How did he reach the conclusion Jenkins was a first-round pick? Who convinced him a team could win a Super Bowl with Bono? Why did he wait until Elliott ruined Marty's best team and best coaching job before admitting his mistake? And why would he dangle a talented quarterback in front of the public and, more important, his players when he knew he wouldn't make a legitimate bid for the QB's services?

■

This defeat magnifies
Schottenheimer's loss of control
November 9, 1998

*The 1998 season will forever be a black mark in Chiefs'
history. Picked by many to go the Super Bowl (and by
some to go undefeated; see Chapter 5) the team imploded,
finished 7-9, and missed the playoffs. Following a Week 9
loss to the Seahawks, Jason interviewed former Chiefs'
MVP Mark Collins about what was wrong with the team
and then tore into Marty Schottenheimer. One week later
the Chiefs embarrassed the entire franchise on national
TV with the Monday Night Meltdown against Denver.*

SEATTLE - More proof. More evidence that coach Marty
Schottenheimer has lost control of the Chiefs.

That's what Kansas City's 24-12 defeat at the feet and
hands of Seattle's Seahawks provided Sunday. The
Seahawks were inept. They amassed just 202 yards of
offense. They converted just two of 11 third downs.
Quarterback Warren Moon threw two interceptions and
no TD passes.

Still, the Seahawks had Sunday's game sealed by halftime.

Kansas City quarterback Elvis Grbac gave the game away
with an interception just before the break. Seattle line-

backer Darrin Smith ran 26 yards untouched with Grbac's bad throw, putting the Seahawks ahead 24-6.

Grbac's toss cooked the Chiefs and fueled the quarterback controversy between him and Rich Gannon. Schottenheimer, known for his stubbornness, did what he'd previously claimed he couldn't envision doing. He benched Grbac in favor of Gannon.

Following the infamous Monday Night Meltdown Marty Schottenheimer tries to explain what happened

He shouldn't have. The Chiefs aren't going anywhere in 1998. Even if John Elway were their quarterback the rest of the year, the playoffs are a Kansas City pipe dream.

The Chiefs have playoff talent but no chemistry, character, courage or sensible coaching. They're vitamin C-deficient.

"I've never been on a team with this much talent, and I've been on some good teams," said Chiefs guard Glenn Parker, a member of Buffalo's four Super Bowl teams. "But we're not a team. That's obvious."

And that was about as candid a comment as was spoken in a solemn, glazed-eyed Chiefs post-game locker room, where players and coaches sat red-faced staring into space. The most candid and accurate comment regarding the Chiefs came from an outsider, Seattle safety Mark Collins, the Chiefs' MVP in 1996 and a 1997 off-season cut.

"There's no leadership on that team. Marty wanted a bunch of thugs, and that's what he's got," said Collins, who left Sunday's game because of a broken bone in his clavicle.

"Derrick Thomas, Chester McGlockton and Leslie O'Neal — that's three of the biggest egos in the league. There's no leadership. Marcus (Allen) isn't there anymore. I'm gone, no Joe Montana. There's no one there to calm them down."

And for this, and everything else that is wrong with the Chiefs, Schottenheimer deserves the blame. When a team shows absolutely zero improvement week after week, there's only one person worthy of blame, and that's the head coach.

It would be easy to blame this loss — and Kansas City's four-game losing streak — solely on Schottenheimer's decision not to play Gannon ahead of Grbac. But that would be inaccurate and unfair.

The Chiefs threw Sunday's game away as a team. They were flagged for a franchise-record 17 penalties, which broke the six-games-old standard by two.

Schottenheimer has preached and preached against penalties throughout the season.

His players have failed to respond.

"I don't have any doubt the (players) are listening to us (the coaches)," Schottenheimer said when asked whether he has lost control of his team. "No, I don't think we've lost control of our football team. I'm not sure what that (question) means. I have no problem with their attentiveness and their work ethic."

The Chiefs are 4-5, and Denver's undefeated Broncos are headed for Arrowhead Stadium and a Monday night matchup that could and should let the nation in on the unraveling of the Schottenheimer-Carl Peterson regime. Kansas City's sorry, stadium-half-filled, pre-Schotten-heimer-Peterson football era won't protect Schottenheimer forever.

Better coaches than Schottenheimer have been forced out or fired. Jimmy Johnson was forced out of Dallas after winning two Super Bowls. Dan Reeves took Denver to three Super Bowls and was fired. The Patriots let Bill Parcells leave after he took New England to a Super Bowl.

Schottenheimer is an excellent coach. But I'm not sure that we need any more proof to reach the conclusion that he has lost control of this team and that he'll never take Kansas City to a Super Bowl.

■

T.O. needs to hit the books
August 12, 2004

One of Jason's strongest traits is his refusal to let any topic or individual be taboo for criticism. Few topics set him off as much as when black athletes misrepresent their struggles. Jason has always been quick to speak out against athletes who compare their struggles to those of people who have faced real adversity.

Terrell Owens' celebrated comments in the September issue of Playboy Magazine bring to mind a saying my father is fond of repeating: "If it talks like an idiot and acts like an idiot, by golly, it is a spoiled modern-day professional athlete whose fame and riches have warped his brain."

There is absolutely no news in the fact that Owens, the former 49ers receiver and now Philadelphia Eagles rabble-rouser, is homophobic and takes great pleasure in running "gay smack" on his old teammate, current Cleveland quarterback Jeff Garcia.

Owens' intellectual capacity is so obviously limited that I'm surprised he didn't throw out another well-worn diss — that Garcia's "mama wears combat boots."

A debate about Garcia's lifestyle is pointless and would

only serve Owens' misguided motives. But there is fertile territory for discussion in Owens' throwaway line in Playboy about NFL players being treated like "slaves and robots." This is becoming a popular refrain among oppressed African-American NFL players. My favorite NFL star, Warren Sapp, popularized this riff last season after being disciplined by the league office for alleged violations of sportsmanship.

Before these claims of new-millennium slavery get too out of hand, I feel it's necessary to call B.S. on the entire concept.

It's perfectly legitimate for black NFL players to complain about league rules that limit free expression. That is their Constitutional right. In this country, we can complain about anything. But it is borderline insane and totally irresponsible for African-American athletes to toss slavery into the debate. It trivializes one of the great crimes in the history of mankind.

Can you imagine a Jewish person, forbidden from doing the "electric slide" in the end zone or grabbing pom-poms after a big play, claiming rules against taunting and excessive celebrations are akin to the persecution Jews faced during the Holocaust? Can you imagine the uproar in the Jewish community if someone were to trivialize the Holocaust in such a manner?

Terrell Owens quacks like an idiot and acts like one as well.

This offseason, the Eagles signed Owens to a seven-year, $42 million deal with a $10 million signing bonus. T.O. needs to rent the movie "Roots" and get an understanding of the type of lifetime contract that Kunta Kinte signed with Massa Reynolds' family.

When slave hunters declared Kunta eligible for the draft shortly after manhood training, I believe he received deluxe accommodations on a one-way slave ship headed for the States, along with gold chains to wear around his neck, ankles and wrists at the combine; a new name; regular ass-whippings; free cotton-picking training; lessons in Ebonics from Fiddler; and discounted foot surgery. Quite a deal. You can easily see the similarities between the plights of Kunta and T.O.

Commissioner Tagliabue and his gaggle of henchmen should be ashamed of themselves for overseeing the type of oppression being forced upon NFL players each season. Denying these well-paid men the right to dance, pick up hidden cell phones, snatch off their helmets and draw attention to themselves is a form of slavery more insidious than anything Jefferson Davis had in mind.

Combating and coping with this sort of fascism from the commissioner's office explains why T.O. and others can't see the flip side of the argument. They can't see that the stringent rules governing sportsmanship in professional football might be a contributing factor in why the NFL is so marketable.

T.O. and Sapp pointed to the freedom of expression that NBA players have. Well, the NBA wishes it was as strong financially as the NFL. The NBA would kill to have the worldwide image that the NFL has with its fan base. NBA teams seem to be constantly relocating in comparison to the NFL, and NBA franchises don't have near the value that NFL teams do. The NBA employs about one-fifth the number of players that the NFL does.

Yes, Shaq, Kobe and the NBA elite make far more money than the NFL elite. But there are far more professional football players than basketball players making good livings in the United States.

And guess what? The NFL harvests almost all of its talent from U.S. soil, and the majority of it is black U.S. soil. The NBA scours the globe looking for young men to make rich.

T.O. is so stupid, he's willing to bite the very hand that is feeding him and others just like him.

■

Chapter 3

Just Because They're Selling Your Jersey Doesn't Mean You're Getting Any Money: The Conflicts and Struggles of College Athletics

Clarett shouldn't suffer alone
September 12, 2003

In 2002 Ohio State running back Maurice Clarett had one of the best seasons ever by a freshman running back, and his two touchdowns in the Fiesta Bowl helped the Buckeyes to their first national title in 34 years. He then had one of the most scandalous off-seasons in college football. On September 10, 2003, Ohio State announced he was suspended for the entire season.

Let's take Ohio State University at its word. Maurice Clarett is a bad dude, a spoiled, pampered, lying, manipulative running back lusting to flout NCAA rules.

Most — or all — of it is a reasonable conclusion to draw from what we've learned about Clarett since the time he carried Ohio State University to its first mythical national championship in decades. He allegedly lied to the police, his university and the NCAA.

But if this is true — Clarett being a teenager and all — why are none of the adults who brought this desperado to Ohio State University suffering from Clarett's many alleged transgressions?

Citing numerous NCAA ethical violations and thousands of dollars of illegal benefits, Ohio State announced

Wednesday it was suspending its star running back for the entire 2003 season. The decision is intended to head off a heavy NCAA penalty and demonstrate that Ohio State University has institutional control of its athletic department.

I don't view Clarett as a victim. He's an immature kid with questionable ethics and character. He spent his free time hobnobbing with LeBron James and is upset that he couldn't enjoy James' financial freedom.

We all do it. We all covet our neighbor's toys. Clarett wants to drive a Hummer far more than he wants an education, which isn't all that surprising given his age.

But what bothers me about this whole situation is that Jim Tressel, the Buckeyes' football coach, and Andy Geiger, the athletic director, won't suffer from the Clarett affair. To the contrary, Maurice Clarett was good for Tressel and Geiger.

Geiger and Tressel can talk all they want about how Clarett's actions tarnished Ohio State's image, but we know otherwise. Clarett helped win Ohio State a national championship, which immeasurably enhanced the school's image.

Take this to Tressel's and Geiger's banks. If they knew then what they know now, Maurice Clarett would still take the field against the Miami Hurricanes in the Fiesta Bowl.

Clarett is nothing more than Ohio State's sacrificial lamb to the NCAA. He committed several of his violations in 2002, while Ohio State was completing its undefeated season. But Ohio State won't forfeit its national title. Why?

Because it's all about money. It's all about donations to the university. It's all about Ohio State University protecting its image as a football powerhouse rather than protecting its integrity as an academic institution first and its integrity for fair play.

Ohio State used Maurice Clarett. You can't tell me that Tressel didn't know what type of person he brought to Ohio State.

Coaches know everything because players squeal. When I was at Ball State, the veteran players ran a starter off the team because they complained that he smoked too much weed. It's easy for an interested coach to get a feel for his players' lifestyles, particularly a coach's star player.

Ohio State wanted a national championship more than it wanted to avoid the kind of controversy it is enduring now.

What's problematic for the NCAA is that Clarett's football-playing, teen-age peers are sympathetic to Clarett's plight. They see the hypocrisy.

This whole situation does nothing more than create more

Maurice Claretts, more college athletes who don't believe in the NCAA system of justice. The system can't survive if all of its participants are non-believers.

■

Huskers' trouble is everyone's
September 14, 1995

Police arrested Nebraska tailback Lawrence Phillips on September 10, 1995, for an assault on his then girlfriend. Phillips' off-field troubles are the biggest black mark against Tom Osborne and his Nebraska program. Phillips never cleaned up his act, bombed in the NFL and the Canadian league and in mid-2004 pawned one of his National Championship rings for $20 while in Las Vegas.

You look at Lawrence Phillips, Heisman Trophy favorite, and you wonder: How could someone with a future so promising be so irresponsibly stupid?

You look at Tom Osborne, legendary coach, and you wonder: How could a man of such strong character and integrity run a program that houses two suspected batterers and one suspected attempted murderer?

You look at the University of Nebraska, last season's No. 1 team, and you wonder: How can a school with a program long viewed as ideal be this deep in controversy and criminal activity?

The answers, check that, the answer is easy.

In the world of NCAA Division I football and men's basketball, there are no sainted schools, there are no saints. There are only would-be saints trapped in corrupt and hypocritical environments, forced to compromise noble principles to satisfy the NCAA's and their university's thirst for the almighty dollar.

To make a long story short: The embarrassing news coming out of Nebraska this week — and throughout the summer — could be generated at any one of the 108 Division I football schools across this great country.

Lawrence Phillips' mug shot following his September 1995 arrest.

As the cliche goes, Nebraska isn't alone.

There are Lawrence Phillipses — undisciplined, uncontrollable, unbrained players — at Ball State, Kansas, Notre Dame, UCLA and everywhere in between.

There are Tom Osbornes — sainted coaches just one bad break from being exposed — at Bowling Green, Kansas State, Michigan, USC and everywhere in between.

And there are Nebraskas — proud universities with dirty sporting secrets — in Ypsilanti, Mich.; Columbia, Mo.; Columbus, Ohio; College Station, Texas; and in all cities between.

That's the truth about big-time college athletics.

I say that not just because of what I experienced as a college athlete at Ball State, which is on the low end of big-time Division I football. I say that because of what I experienced and because of what my friends experienced at the highest levels of college football and on down to bad I-AA football.

It's all the same.

In the pursuit of victories, dollars and better jobs, well-intentioned coaches and universities overlook and cover up steroid use, drinking problems, academic fraud and criminal activity.

Across the country, short suspensions are doled out for "violations of team rules" when a coach has a pretty good suspicion that his player was involved in a serious crime but he's equally sure that charges will never be brought and reporters will never learn about it.

And if you consider the hypocritical minefield we, the media, have coaches operating in, it's not difficult to understand why they sometimes overlook an important player's misdeeds.

Those of us in the media are steadfast in our effort to put more pressure on college coaches — for years we've campaigned for a football playoff — and we're steadfast in our effort to publish investigative stories about corruption and misbehavior when coaches make mistakes trying to stay a step ahead of the ever-increasing pressure.

Before I leave you with the impression that college sports is an evil empire worthy of destruction, let me say this. Coaches are wonderful people, and they generally positively influence young people. Ninety percent of the athletes are fine human beings. (The percentage drops to 50 at the University of Miami.)

It's just that every school has that troublesome 10 percent. It's only a matter of time before that 10th shines an embarrassing light. Nebraska's time is now.

Your favorite university may be next.

■

The farce is with us in colleges
February 22, 2004

On April 28, 2003, The Des Moines Register ran a series of photos of Iowa State head coach Larry Eustachy drinking and flirting with students at a party in Columbia, Mo. The next several months were some of the most scandalous and shocking in college sports, especially for the Big 12: the sex scandal and rape allegations at Colorado, the Ricky Clemons saga at MU, Ell Roberson being accused of rape at the Fiesta Bowl, and the murder investigation at Baylor.

End the hypocrisy, please. The scandals rocking the Big (Southwest) 12 Conference are a cry for help.

Big-time college athletics are rotting from unchecked hypocrisy. You can waste your emotion and time vilifying Colorado and Gary Barnett, Baylor and Dave Bliss, Missouri and Ricky Clemons, Kansas State and Bill "Ell" Snyder and Iowa State and Larry Eustachy.

You can pretend the Big (Southwest) 12 is the only super conference trapped in a sea of unethical behavior. Or you can join me in the realization that college athletics has completely lost its soul. The pursuit of bigger and bigger TV and shoe contracts has eroded college athletics' ethics to the point that it's virtually impossible to run a clean program.

Oh, we, sports fans, buy the myths. We believe Duke and Northwestern and a few others do things the right way. But do we really? Or do we just believe they do things better than everyone else?

Hypocrisy is a lot like pregnancy. You can't be a little bit pregnant and you can't be a little bit hypocritical.

Big-time college athletics calls for a significant percentage of its participants to pretend that they're interested in a college education. That's the original sin that breeds the plethora of sins that make headlines across the country.

You want to know what can be done to address the problems currently being exposed at Colorado?

Do away with the original sin. End the hypocrisy. Quit demanding that football and basketball players pretend to be students. Let them be what they are — entertainers, professional athletes in training.

This would free coaches to be honest.

University of Miami football coach Larry Coker wouldn't have to claim that his latest hotshot recruit, linebacker Willie Williams, is coming to campus to get an education. Once Williams is released from jail — after his 11th arrest — he should be able to join Coker's program without putting on a charade about interest in education.

You see, once the charade begins it takes many other charades to camouflage the original one. You can't tell just one lie.

Answering to curators and regents has become a common event for coaches and AD's; here University of Missouri System President Elsom Floyd discusses the Ricky Clemons situation with the MU Board of Curators.

Colorado is investigating whether Gary Barnett participated in covering up rape allegations against one of his players. A member of Colorado's board of regents told me that alleged act might cost Barnett his job...not Barnett's statements about kicker Katie Hnida.

If it's true, you know what primarily provoked Barnett's cover-up? He has to pretend that he's recruiting nothing but wholesome, boy-next-door young men to Colorado's campus. He has to create the appearance that he's built an ideal, family-values football program, one worthy of Mother Teresa's kiss of approval.

Pro football teams don't have to have a social conscience.

If Dick Vermeil wants to impede the progress of women — and, in his mind, avoid potential problems — and not have a female kicker on his squad, he can do it without regrets or controversy.

If Marty Schottenheimer decides he wants to pursue a championship with Andre Rison, Tamarick Vanover, Bam Morris, Chester McGlockton and a cast of malcontents, he's free to do it without answering to a group of college professors worried about academic or moral integrity.

College coaches deserve this liberating freedom. We're never going to get the money out of college sports, so I'm not going to waste time calling for a de-emphasis of the games. The Ivy League doesn't make money.

So why not pay college athletes to entertain? Let the recruited athletes decide whether they want an academic scholarship or a paycheck. This would end the hypocrisy that is driving a great deal of the corruption. Academic fraud would be less necessary. So would financial fraud. The athletes would have their beer, pizza, laundry, movie and weed money.

Once coaches clear their heads from the haze of half-truths they're currently forced to tell, then perhaps they'll react more ethically and righteously when faced with an allegation of criminal activity hours before their first BCS bowl game. Hypocrisy is a very slippery slope. As long as we continue buying into the myth of "student athlete," the scandals will continue. Until college athletics moves to a platform in which it can be honest with its participants and supporters, we're foolish to expect honesty and integrity from its coaches and players.

Gary Barnett is trapped inside the belly of the beast. Slay the beast, not its prey.

■

It's time for NCAA to put athletes first
March 18, 1999

One of the biggest headaches for the NCAA has always been eligibility standards. The original standards were set by Proposition 48, then replaced in 1995 by Proposition 16, which was struck down in 1999. Currently the NCAA uses a sliding scale that requires an SAT score of 1010 for students with a 2.0 GPA (minimum allowed). Students with a 3.55 or above GPA need only a 400 on the SAT.

Maybe now the NCAA will address the real problem. But I doubt it.

Maybe now that a level-headed Philadelphia judge has

struck down NCAA Proposition 16, which required fresh-man athletes to meet minimum SAT and ACT scores, the NCAA will create a rule that will really help its student-athletes excel in the classroom.

I'm not holding my breath.

Prop 16 has never been more than an NCAA-mandated public-relations ploy, an attempt to convince the news media that the NCAA is interested in its athletes graduating from college.

I'm sure the NCAA will hatch another ploy.

But if the NCAA were really concerned about the gradua-tion rates and educational experiences of its athletes, it would come up with rules that address what happens with its athletes once they hit campus rather than what happened while the athletes were in high school and not under NCAA control.

Get it?

SAT and ACT scores track the progress of students while they were in high school. High school playing fields aren't level. Some kids go to schools with the latest computer equipment, well-trained, decently paid teachers, top-of-the-line facilities and books and in secure environments. Other kids don't.

It's not fair.

Most kids have very little control over the first 18 years of their life. They don't choose their parents, their parents' educational level, their parents' occupations or income level.

And while much of the talk about Prop 16 has focused on whether standardized tests are racially biased, the real truth is that standardized tests discriminate against the poor. I did a research paper on this issue while I was a student at Ball State University. Household income is the key indicator in success or failure on the SAT and ACT, not race.

Let me repeat this for those of you who don't understand what rules America.

Follow the M-O-N-E-Y, not race, when you wonder about achievement on standardized tests. (This rule applies to just about everything that happens in American society.)

For the most part, middle class and wealthy black people don't have any problem with the SAT or ACT. Poor people — white and black — struggle with the tests.

This isn't a secret. But everyone acts as if it is.

Now, I've gone into this before, but it's worthy of being repeated. I'm the product of two supportive, hard-working, stable, black parents who saw to it that I attended an excellent high school and grew up in a safe environment. Without any preparation and without taking the test seriously, I scored a 900 on the SAT, which isn't a great score, but it more than meets freshman eligibility requirements.

Keith "DOC" Stalling, one of my best friends from college, grew up in one of Chicago's toughest housing projects. His mother was just a teenager when she bore Keith. For Keith, getting to school each day was a dangerous adventure through rival gang territory. Keith's high school experience was dramatically different than mine.

Keith scored horribly on the SAT and ACT. He was a Prop 48/16 basketball player at Ball State, meaning he was ineligible as a freshman.

He graduated from Ball State in five years. He works for a large insurance company in Chicago. He owns a home. He's a shining role model in his family, the first to attend college.

There was nothing the NCAA could do to change Keith's childhood. He deserved the opportunity to attend college.

The NCAA should come up with rules that make it possible for its student-athletes to spend more time just being regular students. The time demands on athletes have more to do with low graduation rates than SAT scores.

I wouldn't mind if the NCAA enacted a rule that required borderline students to attend summer school before their freshman seasons. Make Johnny Fullback take 12 hours of freshman-level English, math and history and prove that he's a legitimate college student.

And if the NCAA really wanted to prove it was serious about education, it would make freshmen ineligible. But a decision like that might cost the NCAA a little M-O-N-E-Y.

■

College football is just fine
January 5, 1995

For years there has been argument from most members of the national media for a playoff system to determine the national champion in college football. This was Jason's first column speaking out against a playoff system. At a time when voices around the country were calling for a change, Jason argued that college football is unique because it is the only sport where every game matters.

You know what I never hear?

I never hear one of those college football national playoff whiners articulate why a Division I playoff is so important.

Oh, yes, they rant about the injustice of it all. Poor little Penn State, 12-0, with a terrific coach, a fancy tailback and a gutsy quarterback but no No. 1 ranking.

It's criminal, they say. Why can't the Nittany Lions meet the Nebraska Cornhuskers, they cry.

I just want one of them to tell me why it's so important that they meet.

Is there something called Post Traumatic Non-No. 1-Ranking Stress Disorder that the rest of us know nothing about?

Are the Nittany Lions' Ki-Jana Carter and Kerry Collins likely to spend the rest of their lives strung out on drugs because a bunch of mustard-stained sportswriters didn't pick Penn State No. 1?

Will Joe Paterno tattoo his body, divorce his wife and for the rest of his life sit on a bar stool and bitterly deride America because a bunch of hypocritical coaches didn't recognize his team as the best?

Is that what happens? Is that why a playoff system is so important?

I don't think so. But maybe I'm wrong.

You know what else I never hear?

I never hear one of those college football national playoff whiners articulate the ramifications of a playoff system.

It all sounds so easy today. Give Nebraska and Penn State — the Nos. 1 and 2 teams — two weeks, then have them meet in a college Super Bowl. Voila. Instant justice.

It ain't that easy.

The beauty of Division I college football is that every game is significant.

Every Saturday there's a reason to sit by your radio, sit through the cold, the rain, the fat guy with his knee in your back. Even in sure victories — take for instance Penn State's close victory over Indiana — the final score is significant because it can cost your team ratings points.

Can any of the other major sports — NBA, NFL, major-league baseball, college basketball, NHL — say each of their games is important? No.

That's what makes college football unique.

Well, if you institute a college football playoff, you will not only destroy the importance of regular-season games, you will end a lot of the intriguing, competitive games that make the college season so memorable.

College football would resemble college basketball of the 1980s — Cupcake City. Southwestern Louisiana, Rice and UNLV would not only be on Bill Snyder's schedule, they would be the homecoming date for every school with a national title hope.

Colorado would have no incentive to travel to Ann Arbor, Mich., and face the Wolverines. Does anyone remember that game this season? Does anyone remember Florida State-Notre Dame two years ago?

If there's a playoff, those games are less likely to happen. Schools, particularly the traditional national powers that start each season ranked in the top 10, would try to set up an easy non-conference schedule to position themselves for the playoffs.

There's absolutely nothing wrong with college football — on the field — the way it is today. Even the Carquest Bowl was exciting.

A great philosopher, probably Forrest Gump, once said: "If it ain't broke, don't fix it."

Well, until I see Joe Paterno with a skull-and-crossbones

tattoo and a joint hanging out of his mouth, I'm going to keep believing college football is fine.

■

No thanks, NBA
July 6, 2004

By a quirk of fate Jason was in Durham when news broke that the L.A. Lakers were pursuing Mike Krzyzewski to replace Phil Jackson as head coach. While members of the media around the country speculated on what would happen, Jason was close enough to see what really took place: a shakedown of the university by a coach looking to strengthen his own position.

DURHAM, N.C. — It was a shakedown worthy of a "Sopranos" episode.

Don Mike Krzyzewski, head of the all-powerful Tobacco Road family, consigliore David Falk and underboss Joe Alleva took Duke University's five-day-old president

Richard Brodhead to the cleaners, and Brodhead still has no idea that a credit card is missing from the wallet he left in his slacks. Nor does he care.

Don K's heist was so clean and so deceptive that even the bosses of college basketball's other families are unaware that his shakedown ultimately taxed all of their points.

Early Monday evening inside Cameron Indoor Stadium, after an alleged "serious" flirtation with the Los Angeles Lakers, Coach K listened to the school president he barely knows gush about his integrity and his importance to Duke, and gloat about the world's good fortune that Mike Krzyzewski won't be leaving amateur athletics.

The whole thing just made you feel warm and fuzzy.

Unless you've watched one too many reruns of the Sopranos, or were curious about whether any money exchanged hands.

"We were able to do a few things for Mike in his contract," mumbled Alleva, Duke's athletic director, when asked whether the "lifetime" contract Don K signed in 2001 had been modified.

Before I go any further, let me state quite clearly that I think Coach K is awesome for college athletics. He's an outstanding coach, a true leader and someone of high character. He's as good as it gets in big-time athletics.

But this affair with the Lakers now seems very orchestrated, choreographed, put together. It was a well-timed score.

One year after North Carolina lavished Roy Williams with a perk$-laden contract, not long after the ACC made a huge commitment to football, just weeks after his two best players jumped to the NBA and during Brodhead's first week on the job, suddenly Coach K, the face of college basketball, wants to contemplate a move to LA.

At least now we know Quin Snyder got it honestly.

"The decision has always been to stay at Duke," Coach K said Monday.

Nope. He was never on the brink of taking the Los Angeles job offer his superagent, David Falk, arranged. Falk is the NBA's version of Scott Boras. You see, everyone thinks Kobe Bryant pulled the string to get Coach K in the LA mix. I say it's the work of Falk. Coach K didn't want the job. He just wanted the highly public offer and the terms of the proposed agreement leaked.

Alleva legitimized the offer last Thursday by holding a news conference that Coach K conveniently didn't attend. A real Don never gets his hands dirty.

"There wasn't a negative that prompted this," Coach K said when asked whether the early player defections in college basketball made him consider moving to the pros. "One of the reasons I coach is because of the challenges."

Hmmm. Last week when Alleva — who has worked with Krzyzewski for all of Coach K's 24 years at Duke — was fueling the flames that Coach K was L.A.-bound, the athletic director insinuated quite strongly that Krzyzewski was frustrated by the early defections.

"The state of college basketball is not the greatest in the world," Alleva said last week when asked what might motivate Coach K to jump. "And I'm sure that's frustrating when you recruit a kid and they don't show up and you recruit a kid and they come for one year and leave. That's frustrating."

Alleva left you with the impression that he wasn't speculating about Krzyzewski's feelings.

"I've had a lot of conversations with (Coach K) in the last few days," Alleva said last week. "He has meant so much for Duke and college basketball that obviously we're going to try to do everything we can to keep him in college basketball."

Monday, Alleva wouldn't be specific about what Duke did to keep Coach K. When asked directly about a new practice facility, Alleva said: "We were going to do that anyway."

What about new contracts for Coach K's assistants?

"No," Alleva said, appearing disturbed by the question.

Did the assistant coaches get pay raises?

Alleva looked at me and walked away.

It was a great score. It was old-school. Coach K never raised his voice or his hand, but he let his new president know exactly who runs things on Tobacco Road. He also sent a similar message to basketball recruits across the land: Coach K is the unquestioned king of amateur hoops. Check "SportsCenter" and USA Today if you doubt it.

Think about it. Coach K, without uttering a word or meeting face-to-face with owner Jerry Buss, had us all believing he might uproot his family and move to the West Coast for the privilege of coaching a young man who is scheduled to stand trial for rape this year.

I feel stupid for falling for it. Brodhead shouldn't. He had no other choice.

■

Don't pay college athletes
March 14, 1995

The topic of compensation for college athletes has always been a tricky one. At times Jason has argued that schools should stop pretending to care about the academic welfare of their athletes and just pay them for their services. But as a former Division I scholarship athlete he also knows the potential benefits for people who take advantage of the opportunity. In this column he argues the chance at a free education is payment enough.

College athletes should not be paid or given a stipend.

Read that sentence again.

It's important because Monday night, if you watched ESPN's "Outside the lines" investigative piece on NCAA basketball, you might have been brainwashed into believing poor little Jacque and poor little Greggy were being financially exploited by the NCAA.

ESPN's hourlong look at college basketball and the money its NCAA tournament produces was designed to lend credence to the biggest myth circulating in college sports: American amateur athletes are starving, and it's all the fault of the stingy, oppressive and exploitive NCAA.

I could just hear college athletes around the country screaming in unison, "Give me beer and pizza money, or give me death!"

Well, I'm here to say stop the liberal, out-of-touch, I-feel-your-pain whining.

The bellyaching about underprivileged, non-working-by-NCAA-mandate scholarship athletes is a joke, and it's a product of an uninformed media and a society full of people who want everything handed to them. We're a nation that can't spell sacrafise, uh, sacrafize, well, you know what I mean.

College athletics certainly has its flaws, but a lack of financial compensation for athletes isn't one of them.

Our very own Kansas Jayhawks participated in the whine-off. ESPN used KU basketball players Jacque Vaughn and Greg Ostertag to make its point, explaining that Kansas profits between $3 million and $4 million a year from its hoop program while Jacquey and Greggy supposedly go hungry.

It's a lie.

"No one says athletes should be paid," said ESPN's Greg Garber — who interviewed the KU players and Coach Roy Williams — when I reached him by phone Monday afternoon. "The question we ask is whether there should be a small stipend to pay for incidentals."

"You take a guy like Greg Ostertag. He has a wife and a kid."

Unless the NCAA walked down the aisle and said, "I do," unless the NCAA impregnated Ostertag's wife, Ostertag's family situation has nothing to do with whether the NCAA should pay its athletes.

All Kansas and the NCAA owe Ostertag is an opportunity to obtain an education. That, as hard as it may be to fathom, is a very fair exchange. And despite what you may read in the newspaper or see on TV, 99.9 percent of America's universities are providing jocks with ample opportunity to get a degree.

I have never known or heard of a college athlete who really wanted a degree not getting one. I know plenty who have talked of getting a degree but never put the 40-ounce or joint or cheerleader down long enough to obtain one.

The other thing that really annoys me about this entire debate is how the media portray athletes (or allow athletes to portray themselves) as starving Bosnians.

"We can't eat every time we're hungry," one idiotic New

Mexico State basketball player said.

Does this bozo really believe he's the only college student who can't order a pizza every time he gets the inkling?

There are very few college students who don't eat an unusual amount of macaroni and cheese or who don't go to bed hungry some nights because they mismanaged their money.

Athletes live as good as the majority of college students. And if you judge by designer clothes and gold jewelry, then I'd say athletes live better than the average student.

But what do I know compared with ESPN?

■

Chapter 4

Once Upon a Time You Just Had to Be Good: The Influence and Evolution of Big Business and Sports

Why keep Straw out of a job?
June 14, 1995

Darryl Strawberry was National League Rookie of the Year in 1983, won a World Series ring in 1986, and was an All-Star eight times. In 1994 he admitted to substance-abuse problems and entered treatment. The next decade would see Strawberry float in and out of baseball playing for three teams, winning two World Series, failing three drug tests, and twice having surgery for colon cancer. After his first failed drug test, he was signed by the Yankees in 1995, a move that drew much criticism. In this column Jason fires back at those critics and calls them out as hypocrites.

Darryl Strawberry deserves every chance he gets.

The double standard that the news media have set up for athletes and that society (all the way down to the Didn't-Inhale Clinton administration) seems to have bought into infuriates me.

The fact there is a debate about whether Strawberry, once the most-promising outfielder in baseball, should be allowed to work again as a major-leaguer strikes me as ridiculous.

Strawberry, now a minor-leaguer for George Steinbrenner's Yankees, isn't a murderer. He's not a child molester or rapist or arsonist or drug dealer. And if evading taxes was all it took for a person to lose his right to work, America would shut down.

Here's what Strawberry is: one of the many million Americans — the overwhelming majority of whom don't even play sports recreationally — ignorant enough to try illegal drugs, like them and then become addicted to them.

And for that crime, I'm not ready to tell a person that they don't deserve a second, third, fourth, fifth, sixth or seventh chance. They deserve every chance they get, and every time they attempt to recover from their addiction they deserve our support — not scorn.

Anyone who has had a family member or loved one addicted to drugs knows what I'm talking about. Those of you lucky enough to have never faced such a crisis, trust those of us who have.

But, judging from the reaction of the Yankees' signing of Strawberry, many of you appear ready to banish Strawberry to a life without baseball, his chosen, perfectly legal profession.

President Didn't Inhale's national drug policy director, Lee Brown, even criticized Steinbrenner, claiming Strawberry's signing sent the wrong message to kids.

"If you use drugs, you can be rewarded with big money in big-time sports," is what Brown said the message was to kids.

That line of thinking is so stupid and simplistic that I hate wasting time responding to it. And it certainly isn't the message that Strawberry's signing sends. (If it were, I'd suggest everybody pick up a crack pipe and head down to Kauffman Stadium.)

I'm not sure there is any significant message in Strawberry's rehiring. It really only confirms what has been obvious ever since George Washington crossed the Delaware River:

In a capitalistic society, if you have money-producing talent, other capitalists will help you realize your potential.

But if Strawberry were permanently banned from pursuing the profession of his choice, the message would be clear:

This is a hypocritical society intent — for some unknown reason — on holding athletes to a standard of conduct that the rest of society doesn't have to reach.

All the people clamoring for Strawberry to be banned from baseball have yet to articulate what profession he should pursue.

Is it OK for taxi drivers to be drug users? Or should he work at Burger King? Or maybe they think he should go back to school and become a doctor? Or maybe he should take up a career as an entertainer?

Yeah, we don't seem to mind if actors or musicians are strung out on drugs and alcohol.

Hank Williams Jr. can come to Kansas City drunker than Mickey Mantle, charge people $30, sing a song, curse the audience and walk offstage without anyone asking for him to be banned from the music industry.

Unless we're all ready to play by the same rules, I suggest everybody shut up and pray that Strawberry has a long-lasting sobriety.

■

Win or lose, it's ratings that count

July 15, 2001

Over the past decade television networks have pumped more and more money into sports and have tried to exert more and more influence to increase their marketing potential. Jason looks at the factors driving sports today.

Big-time sports in America has a new final score. Well, actually, it's not all that new. It's just that many of us are just now coming to the realization that it's the only score that really matters to the people who really matter.

And once you reach this realization, the assertion that the outcome of competitive sports might be manipulated or influenced won't seem farfetched.

The new final score isn't shown on any stadium or arena scoreboard. It doesn't have a betting line — yet. It has nothing to do with how many points Shaquille O'Neal scores, how many passes Tony Gonzalez catches or how many home runs Barry Bonds hits.

Big-time sports in America isn't about who wins or loses the game. It's about how many people tune in to watch on television. The final score is generally revealed a day or two after the game/match/race when the TV ratings are announced. That's when the people who really matter, the people who run professional sports leagues, decide whether the Super Bowl, NBA finals, Daytona 500, the Masters or Wimbledon were successful or not.

That's when they decide what needs to be fixed.

Oops. I don't mean "fixed" as in rigged. I mean "fixed" as in presented in a more viewer-friendly, ratings-enhancing style.

What I'm saying isn't at all new. Television has been in control of big-time sports for quite some time. What's new is the realization that TV's control might infringe upon the integrity of the outcome of the sporting events it pays billions of dollars to broadcast.

We've grown accustomed to TV dictating the starting time of events, the lengthening of halftime extravaganzas, the intrusion of Dennis Miller on NFL games.

But we're just now seriously exploring the possibility that in an effort to satisfy its new television partner, NBC, NASCAR might have given Dale Earnhardt Jr. a competitive advantage in last week's Pepsi 400, the first race at Daytona International Speedway since Earnhardt Jr.'s father died there in February.

We're also questioning Cal Ripken's home run at the All-Star Game. The high fastball that Ripken torpedoed was a "retirement gift" from pitcher Chan Ho Park. In my mind, the grooved pitch wouldn't have been a big deal if commissioner Bud Selig hadn't stopped the game after the fifth inning for a made-for-TV tribute to Ripken and Tony Gwynn.

Everything is about TV ratings. So why not the outcome?

The same TV executives who are now in control of big-time sports are the same people in control of "Survivor" and the reality-TV craze. Wasn't the outcome of "Survivor" influenced?

In the world of sports, NASCAR and Tiger Woods are the only events with ascending TV ratings. Everything else, with the possible exception of the NFL, is going in the toilet. There are just too many cable channels to maintain the super-high ratings, to justify the multibillion-dollar contracts for sporting events.

NASCAR invented restrictor-plate racing (43 somewhat evenly matched cars running in a pack) to make its sport more TV-friendly. Every time Tiger runs off a string of dominant victories, PGA Tour courses consider restrictor-fairway tournaments (Tiger-proof courses) in hopes that three or four golfers can hang with Tiger.

(FYI: The pursuit of TV ratings will eventually break the NCAA. That organization will come up with a way to pay its best men's college basketball players to stem the tide of early NBA defections.)

Before the Pepsi 400, NBC told NASCAR's drivers they needed to smile more and show some emotion for the cameras. According to script, Earnhardt Jr. turned doughnuts in the infield, hopped on the hood of his car and dived into the arms of his supporters.

You could hear the cash registers and TV ratings ringing as Little E celebrated.

I have no idea if Earnhardt Jr. had a competitive advantage over the other drivers. In the final laps, his car showed an uncanny amount of power for a restrictor-plate race. I do know it was the perfect ending for television. I do know that even the competitors are beginning to question the integrity of the games we watch on TV.

I also know that the people who matter the most know that when it comes to television viewership the integrity of the outcome doesn't really matter. The participants, the support personnel, the league executives and the television networks can all get rich as long the journey to the climax looks real.

■

Big-league concern: Baseball has stake in price of Royals
July 18, 1998

On August 1, 1993, Royals' founder and owner Ewing Kauffman passed away, setting off one of the most frustrating and complicated ownership transfers in sports' history. Five years after his death a board selected to oversee the sale of the franchise was negotiating a price with interested buyers. During this crucial period in Royals' history Jason used his national ties to speak with three of the most important figures in baseball.

One thing I may have miscalculated in my assessment of the stalemate over the sale of the Royals is Major League Baseball's interest in the price of the club.

Many of the leaders of Major League Baseball don't believe it's in the best interest of baseball for Kansas City's franchise to sell for less than $75 million, the stated minimum purchase price. If the Royals sell cheaply, it could affect the future asking price of other small-market clubs such as Pittsburgh or Montreal or Cincinnati. (Or try to understand it this way: It's like building and owning a $300,000 house and finding out your next-door neighbor is selling his house for $175,000. You ain't happy.)

And as for image, the Royals selling for, let's say, $55

million would be a black eye for professional baseball.

My point: In an earlier column, I stated that Mike Herman and the Royals' board of directors are trying to avoid being run over by the Lamar Hunt/Western Resources group, which I still believe is partly true. But I now believe (and have learned) that Herman and the board also are being pressured by Major League Baseball to stand firm at $75 million.

Friday I called commissioner Bud Selig, American League president Gene Budig and New York Yankees owner George Steinbrenner to ask them Major League Baseball's position on the Royals' sale price. Shockingly, they all returned my calls.

"It is important that any of our franchises draw a fair price. It's in the best interest of the game," Budig responded when I asked him whether major-league owners were pressuring Herman.

So I asked Budig again, a little differently.

Would major-league owners be upset if the Royals were sold for less than $75 million?

"It's important that the Royals draw a fair price," Budig said, "because that would impact them (the other owners)."

Newly appointed commissioner Selig was adamant in stating that major-league owners aren't trying to influence the price of the Royals.

"Absolutely not," Selig barked almost before I finished the question. "We have great faith in David Glass and Mike Herman."

Budig and Selig were helpful.

But I called Steinbrenner because I knew he would be bluntly honest.

"Yes, there might be some people upset if the franchise sold too cheaply," said Steinbrenner, who was in Florida on a business trip. "I would always love to see baseball in Kansas City. I have many fond memories of Ewing Kauffman and Muriel and the competition between the Royals and the Yankees ... "

Steinbrenner continued his walk down memory lane. Eventually, I stopped him and got him back on track.

"If it does (sell cheaply), that would certainly reflect," Steinbrenner said and then paused to gather his thoughts.

After a few seconds, he made this enlightening statement: "One of the biggest things a commissioner can do for a league is to increase the value of the franchises of the franchise owners. Certainly David Stern has been a master at it with the NBA and all the things they've done.

"Certainly Paul Tagliabue has done it for football. Certainly hockey is doing it."

That sounds like pressure to me. That sounds like the new commissioner's most important job is to increase the value of major-league franchises.

And the first franchise on the auction block during Selig's weeklong, official rulership of Major League Baseball is our money-losing, small-market Royals.

That's a tough spot.

But I guess we — those of us who want Hunt to buy the Royals — should take comfort in the fact that at the end of my conversation with Steinbrenner, the Yankees owner said all the right things.

"Mike Herman and David Glass and the people running the (Kauffman) Foundation should do as they please," Steinbrenner said. "If it bothers baseball, so what? It's a man's right to run the foundation the way he wants."

"They should do whatever is best for the foundation and Kansas City. The league shouldn't be sticking their noses into it."

I agree.

And Herman and the board should ignore the league if it is sticking its nose in our business. Mr. K put the board in position to do what's best for Kansas City, not what's best for baseball.

I have yet to see any overwhelming proof that Hunt isn't what's best for Kansas City.

■

Giving agents their due
July 4, 1995

In the summer of 1995 the NBA players moved to decertify their union. As the negotiations grew worse Jason wrote a column calling sports agents "the dirtiest, filthiest, slimiest group of human beings God ever allowed to walk the earth." That column prompted a phone call from an old (fictitious) friend.

"Jason, you've really done it this time," Laython Zeldon Jerk screamed into the telephone. "You've gone too far. Our friendship is in jeopardy."

That's how my Sunday night conversation began with my longtime friend and old college teammate Lay Z Jerk.

Lay Z lettered in six different sports at Ball State. And, after pocketing more than $30 million in signing bonuses from the NFL, NBA and major-league baseball, in a move he called "Jim Brown-esque," Lay Z retired at the age of 25, before he struck out a batter, recorded a tackle or blocked a shot at the professional level.

Lay Z and I often debate the great sports issues of the day. Sunday he was upset by my mild criticism of sports agents.

"Your column today (Sunday) is absolutely outrageous," Lay Z wailed. "It's ridiculous."

Is that you, Lay Z? I heard you were out of the country vacationing. How'd you see my column today?

"My agent, Harry Handinpocket, faxed it to me. I'm in France with a few of my honeys. You know, the French aren't nearly as sexually repressed as we Americans are."

You mean they have bigger and better nude beaches?

"And you know this, man. But anyway, Jason, back to your totally asinine column. Don't you know that agents are an athlete's best friend? They're freedom fighters, willing to look the man in the eye and say, "Five more million and you've got a deal.' "

"If there weren't any agents, Jason, there would be no such thing as a no-cut contract. If there weren't any agents, unproven rookies wouldn't sign multimillion-dollar deals. Jason, if there weren't any agents, there would still be idiots talking about playing for the love of the game."

Yes, I see. Agents are responsible for the enlightenment of the modern-day athlete.

"You better believe they are. And they're the reason the no-good, worthless owners treat us like human beings."

"I can remember back when I was working out my deal with the Yankees. At that time, the Yankees kept big coolers of water in the dugout. Well, as you know, I have a very sensitive palate. I only drink bottled water. Harry had me sit out spring training until the Yankees agreed to keep bottled mountain water in the dugout."

Hold on, Lay Z. In college, I saw you drink a six pack of Old Milwaukee out of a cheerleader's shoe and drive in six runs the next day.

"Jason, that was in my youth. I was 20 or 21 then. Once you hit your mid-20s, your body takes a downhill turn."

Are you sure it's not your brain that took that turn?

"Real funny, Jason. But like I was saying, agents are the guys who negotiate the important stuff for you. I remember back when I was with the Raiders. Al Davis served sirloin steak for the pre-game meal. As you know, I have a sensitive stomach. Growing up, my mom only prepared the best meat. So Harry had me sit out the first four games of the regular season. The Raiders, after losing four straight, backed down and served me filet mignon the rest of the year."

I can't believe you did that, Lay Z. Your mother might have cooked filet mignon on her job. But I saw your whole family pour A-1 sauce on pork steaks and get in a fistfight over your baby brother's leftover fat.

"There was meat on that fat! And anyway, I didn't call to argue about my past. I called to tell you that when it comes to freedom fighters, sports agents are in a league of their own."

You're so right.

Peterson letting pride get in way of making deal
May 15, 2002

In the summer of 2002 the Chiefs and tight end Tony Gonzalez were involved in a contract dispute. Gonzalez, the former first round pick, was asking for money comparable to what a receiver with his statistics would receive. Carl Peterson was committed to offering little more than what other tight ends around the league were paid. Jason gathered information on the negotiations and published private correspondence that exposed Peterson's manipulation of the issue.

We think of Carl Peterson as a calm, calculated chess player with a temper-control problem. The reality may very well be that Peterson, the president/general manager of the Chiefs, isn't calm or calculated.

He might just be a bully. Nothing more. Nothing less.

How else do we explain his decision to turn the Tony Gonzalez contract negotiations into a public spectacle, complete with CAPITALIZED and underlined emotional outbursts and threats of a personal war with a respected agent?

Peterson couldn't have thought his attack through. It's just mid-May; training camp is two months away. It's not time to panic. This is no time to draw a line in the sandbox.

Following some of the ugliest contract negotiations in Chiefs' history Tony Gonzalez shakes hands with his agent Tom Condon while Carl Peterson walks down the hall.

Gonzalez is the best player Peterson has ever been associated with. Gonzalez is better than Derrick Thomas, Peterson's only other Hall of Fame-caliber draft pick. Gonzalez could wind up being the best tight end ever to play the game. He could wind up as Peterson's signature player.

It makes no sense to go to war with Gonzalez in the middle of May, before the weather turns really hot and coach Dick Vermeil grows legitimately concerned about Gonzalez's status.

So why do it?

"I just hope pride and ego doesn't get in the way of a deal getting done," Gonzalez said at the end of our phone conversation Monday afternoon. "We're all on the same team. We all work for Lamar Hunt. I don't want to play anywhere else. I don't want there to be any hard feelings. That's why

I'm watching what I say."

Gonzalez may have been watching what he said, but by mentioning "pride and ego" he correctly pointed out Peterson's fatal failing. Pride and ego cause Peterson to lose control of his temper. Pride and ego cause him to curse at players and agents who won't negotiate at his pace and on his terms. Pride and ego cause Peterson to sit at his desk and type silly letters to grown men capitalizing and underlining words for emphasis.

Pride and ego — Peterson's — may stand in the way of the Chiefs signing a long-term contract with Gonzalez. That would be a shame. Gonzalez is a truly special player who has earned a monster, standard-setting contract.

Gonzalez is the Randy Moss of tight ends, a freak whose raw talents dwarf his peers. Unlike Moss, Gonzalez's dedication to the game and professionalism is unquestioned. A year ago the Minnesota Vikings dropped a $75-million contract with $18 million (two payments) in signing bonus on Moss, the big-play receiver.

All that matters in the NFL is the signing bonus. Contract negotiations are won in the same spot as the games — upfront.

Peterson and Gonzalez's agent, Tom Condon, might get bogged down in a protracted contract dispute. They're going to fight over $2 million. The Chiefs have offered Gonzalez $8 million to sign. Gonzalez wants $10 million.

He wants $10 million because that's what a receiver with similar statistics as Gonzalez would receive. Peterson won't give it to him because Gonzalez isn't a receiver, and NFL rules stipulate that by using the franchise tag Peterson has every right to treat Gonzalez as a tight end during contract negotiations. League rules say Peterson can pay Gonzalez $3 million this season and not much more the year after that and the year after that and so on and so on.

Peterson is in the right, but he's wrong.

He should pay Gonzalez based on production, not position. You can't really compare Gonzalez's production to other tight ends. He produces at a rate nearly twice as high as the league's other high-priced tight ends.

Does that mean he should earn twice as much? Maybe.

I do know it's pointless to compare him to Jay Riemersma or Mark Bruener or any other traditional tight end.

We've watched Tony play. We know how special he is. We know there's no other tight end like him in the league. We know that when Tony is catching the ball regularly the Chiefs' offense is generally clicking. We know Tony will make things easier for Trent Green and Johnnie Morton and Priest Holmes.

Give him the $2 million just for putting up with Peterson's (stuff).

"I read the story, 'He's hopping mad. He's furious.'" Gonzalez said, referring to the Peterson story. "I'm not mad at all. I learned a long time ago that the art of negotiation is to not take things personal."

"At some point the general manager is going to have to (hack) off a player. But I respect the guy (Peterson). I like the guy. I like working for him. This is all just business."

Someone tell Peterson. He thinks he's battling Godzilla.

Not enough fame to go around
December 5, 2003

The Negro Leagues Baseball Museum was founded in 1990 and is headquartered at 18th and Vine in Kansas City, only a block away from where Rube Foster headed a group that formed the Negro National League in 1920. In December of 2003 a group based in Washington D.C. announced plans to build their own hall of fame for the Negro Leagues. In this piece Jason takes the stance that too often black people hurt themselves and limit their own progress.

No one likes to talk about it around the Negro Leagues Baseball Museum, at least not out loud on the record.

But one of the biggest problems facing the museum is the rampant jealousy directed at Buck O'Neil by other former Negro Leaguers.

They think Buck is making millions of dollars. They're tired of Buck being the celebrated spokesman for the Negro Leagues.

They want a slice of the perceived financial windfall from the sale of Negro League apparel.

So now there are plans to build a Negro League Legends

Hall of Fame in Washington, D.C. This isn't good. It's not right.

The Negro Leagues don't need a second hall of fame/ museum. The one here still needs better support. It's still in its infancy. But there are old black men determined to get a piece of the pie.

"We need this," said Sam Allen, a former Kansas City Monarch, in a story that ran Thursday in The Star. "I've got grandchildren, and I sit them down and tell them, but then they want to see the proof. With this museum coming up, they'll be able to come here and see my name and my picture. It's a long time coming."

Buck O'Neil stands next to a statue of Satchel Paige at the Negro Leagues Baseball Museum. O'Neil's popularity has turned him into the face and voice of the Negro Leagues.

Give me a break. Sam Allen knows full well there's already a museum right here in Kansas City.

I talked with Negro Leagues Museum spokesman Bob Kendrick on Thursday, and he assured me that all of the living former Negro Leaguers have been contacted and made aware of the museum here in Kansas City.

This is about money and petty jealousy. This is about the sale of throwback jerseys and who is and isn't profiting from them.

"These fellows today that make all these big salaries, they could donate something," 88-year-old Sonny Randle was quoted as saying Wednesday. "They could contribute to the older fellows that didn't get a chance."

It would be great if everybody gave back.

Long ago there were black journalists who made far less money than I do today. They paved the way for the freedom and financial security that I enjoy today. Do I owe them money? Or should I take care of my family and give back to the people in this community who support me and The Kansas City Star?

We wonder where these young athletes get their sense of entitlement. Some college athletes feel like they should be compensated because universities profit from the sale of jerseys. Everybody feels like they're owed something.

It's sad that our fledgling museum could get hurt because a bunch of old men are jealous and greedy. Two museums won't survive.

It's difficult enough to retrieve authentic Negro League artifacts. It's difficult enough to raise money to support the museum we have here. It's difficult enough to get current major-leaguers to support our museum.

All of it will become more difficult and more complicated if there are two museums competing for the same dollars, the same artifacts, the same support from current players.

Buck O'Neil volunteered to support Kansas City's museum. It's not a paid position. Yes, Buck is a desired public speaker. He makes a good living doing speaking engagements. He's blessed with a gift. He's a tremendous communicator. Ken Burns' documentary made Buck a star.

It's unfortunate that every living Negro Leaguer doesn't have Buck's gift, or wasn't given the same opportunity as Buck in Burns' documentary.

But that's life. Move on. Support the museum we do have. The money that's going to be spent on the new museum could be used on the one we already have.

This whole fiasco is a prime example of one more thing we black folks don't like to talk about out loud. We have difficulty supporting each other. We refuse to be happy for each other's success. We love to moan and groan about racism. And we avoid combating the stupid, petty, self-destructive things we do to ourselves.

Preserving the legacy of the Negro Leagues isn't about old

players making money off jerseys and bobblehead dolls. It's about preserving history and making sure the players and their contributions to the game and social progress are never forgotten. Too bad the people behind the museum in D.C. don't care.

■

Chapter 5

The Forward Pass Was Not the Most Important Innovation of the Last Century: The Media and Its Impact on Sports

It's time to send a message
April 7, 1995

As major league baseball players prepared to return to the field following the '94 strike, Jason argued that the fans needed to take action and voice their displeasure with the game. In this column he announces the plan for a boycott of Opening Day at Kauffman Stadium. One of the most important impacts Jason has had during his time in Kansas City is getting the fans to speak up and take action. Jason met with acting Royals president Mike Herman and negotiated a settlement of the proposed boycott. The Royals gave their fans close to $500,000 in discounted concessions on Opening Day. The proposed boycott and its outcome was another spark in the feud between Jason and broadcaster Don Fortune.

David Cone, Cy Young Award winner, local hero, one of the best reasons to visit Kauffman Stadium. Gone. Adios. See ya. Traded for a few prospects.

Day 4 of major-league baseball held hostage by the S.O.B.s (Stupid Offensive Baseballers) wasn't any prettier for Royals fans than Day 3, when Brian McRae, center fielder, local hero, one of the best reasons to visit Kauffman Stadium, was traded for a couple of prospects.

It's going to get worse for our small-market, budget-cutting Royals.

As long as the players refuse to compromise, which would mean agreeing to some kind of salary cap, and as long as the big-market owners refuse to compromise, which would mean agreeing to share revenue, you, the fan will be compromised and exploited as always.

Thursday, I asked what you were prepared to do about it, were you ready to send a forceful message to the bozos who put you through nearly 240 days of excruciating pain for nothing.

No sport ever alienated its fans the way MLB did in the nineties. Here a fan yells at players arriving at Kauffman Stadium.

You responded overwhelmingly. My phone rang from 6:40 a.m. until 7 p.m. Of the more than 600 calls I personally answered, only three or four were against taking action.

Caller Calvin Hughes: "I'm in my 60s. I'm old enough to be your grandfather, Jason. And I can tell you that these guys don't care about the guy working in a factory trying to support a family. They don't care. And I don't care if I never see another game."

Caller Debbie: "I feel the same way about returning baseball fans as I do about women who return to men who are beating them senseless and toothless."

Caller Wade Freeman: "I like the idea of a boycott, but I don't think you went far enough. It should be all season, and it should be national."

Here's the tentative plan. Opening Day, April 26, Baltimore at Kansas City. The intelligent men and women of this community who are tired of being taken for granted by whiny players and wimpy owners should stay out of Kauffman Stadium.

Plans are being discussed for an alternate, festive event for People Against S.O.B.s to attend. Radio station KY102 called and offered its support. Many callers suggested that we tailgate in the Kaufman Stadium parking lot. That's not a bad idea. I'll look into it. I'll have more details later.

But today I want to reiterate to you the importance and the reason for our action. The naysayers and the cowards will give you all sorts of reasons why this is a bad idea. Don't listen.

It's time for some tough love.

For the most part, I blame the players for this entire fiasco. They refuse to understand it's in their best interest that small-market teams survive and compete at a high level. I'd love for three or four organizations to fold, which would put about 100 big-leaguers in the unemployment line just so Barry Bonds has the right to make $12 million a year instead of $9 million.

But I'm not absolving the owners, even the small-market ones, of blame totally. They were a part of creating this mess, and they need to be put over our knee and spanked, too.

If you truly love baseball, if you truly love professional sports, you won't pass up this opportunity to send athletes and owners a clear and concise message — you're tired of being used, pimped and exploited. This could be your only opportunity.

Or maybe I've got this whole thing wrong and you enjoy escalating ticket prices with no on-field improvement, players throwing firecrackers at young fans, paying top dollar for the right to have a player sign an autograph and the cancellation of the World Series.

It's about opinions, not biases
December 22, 1998

From 1997-1999 troubled wide-receiver Andre Rison played for the Chiefs. Rison was successful early on in Kansas City and was very popular with fans but quickly wore out his welcome. Following a loss to the Giants in 1998 Rison instigated an explosive encounter with Jason that was caught on camera and replayed continuously on ESPN. This was Jason's response to the incident.

Business should never be personal. That's a philosophy my father ground into my head over and over again when we'd talk about the neighborhood nightclubs he has successfully owned and operated most of my life.

It's a philosophy that I take great pride in adhering to in my job as a newspaper columnist.

Andre Rison, a Chiefs wide receiver, believes that I have been critical of him for some unexplained "personal" reasons. While being restrained by teammates, Rison expressed that to me Sunday after the Chiefs' loss to the Giants.

It's not true.

I do everything in my power to keep my personal feelings from interfering with the opinions and observations that I write in this column. And when I can't keep my personal feelings out of it, I admit it in print.

Take Oakland Raiders quarterback Jeff George. I have never hidden the fact that my childhood friendship with George and his family has slanted my view on his football career. I'm biased when it comes to George, and I don't have any doubt that the bias shows up in the opinions I express about George.

When it comes to the Chiefs, or any of our other hometown teams, I take great pains in removing my personal feelings and just spouting my honest opinions. This is particularly true when I express an opinion about a player's or a team's or a coach's performance.

Personally, I like Derrick Thomas and Marty Schotten-heimer a great deal. I respect the way Thomas has given back to this community. He's a marvelous football player. As for Schottenheimer, up until this year, I was always impressed with his candor and honesty. And I believe he's a tremendous football coach who has been the victim of some incredibly bad breaks.

My fondness for Thomas and Schottenheimer has not pre-vented me from being critical of their job performances. It's my opinion that for the good of both men and the good of the Chiefs organization, it's time for both Schotten-heimer and Thomas to leave the Chiefs.

That's a harsh opinion. Some might consider it "negative." Many people wonder why I seem to write so many "negative" opinions.

I don't consider my opinions to be negative. I do think that I'm more critical than most. That's probably a product of the fact that when I was growing up in Indianapolis, my hometown newspaper was never critical of my favorite sports team, the Indiana Pacers. The Pacers were awful when I was a kid. But the Indianapolis media covered the Pacers as if they were world champions.

The news media seemed more concerned about pleasing the Pacers' players and coaches rather than pleasing me, a lowly newspaper subscriber.

I've never forgotten that feeling. So when I got into this business, I promised myself that I would only concern myself with trying to please newspaper subscribers, not athletes, coaches or front-office types.

It's my opinion that newspaper readers are attracted to honest, agenda-less, unconcerned-with-political-correctness opinions. They may not like them, they may not agree with them, but in the long run they respect and enjoy them.

So that's what I do. Four times a week, I express my honest opinions, which I don't confuse with The Absolute Truth. Only the participants and God know the real truth.

Hip-hop culture is root
of NFL violence
February 3, 2000

*February 2000 saw NFL players in the news for a variety
of serious crimes. Ray Lewis was arrested on Jan 31,
2000, on charges of double murder; on June 5, 2000, he
pleaded guilty to misdemeanor obstruction of justice. Rae
Carruth was arrested for being part of a conspiracy to kill
a woman eight-months pregnant with his child; on January
22, 2001, he was sentenced to 19-24 years in prison. Bam
Morris and Tamarick Vanover were both implicated in a
large-scale drug investigation on January 25, 2000. In the
end Morris pleaded guilty to attempting to distribute over
200 pounds of marijuana and Vanover pleaded guilty to
assisting in the sale of a stolen car. Jason took a controversial stance on what factors contributed to these events,
and the following column drew the ire of local rapper
Tech N9ne and numerous voices throughout the black
community.*

Searching for a reason why crimes committed by football
players are increasing in severity?

This week you have asked yourself over and over again
how could wealthy NFL players Rae Carruth and Ray
Lewis be implicated in murders and how could Bam

Morris and Tamarick Vanover possibly be entangled in a drug-trafficking investigation?

Good questions.

I say the violence and lawlessness that we're witnessing today among black professional athletes is a direct by-product of the popularity of "hip-hop" culture.

Many of you reading this remember the 1960s: hippies, counterculture, an era of loose, wild living. Led by the Doors, the Grateful Dead, and a bunch of other drugged-out rock 'n' rollers and pop-culture icons white kids went wild.

Hip-hop music and culture, a phenomenon of the mid-1980s and 1990s, is no different from what we experienced in the 1960s, except it's a predominantly black culture and its music celebrates, glorifies and promotes violence and lawlessness along with sex, drugs and rap 'n' roll.

I know many of you think it's simple-minded to blame such a complex problem on something as harmless as a music culture.

I'm no fool. I understand that there are tons of factors contributing to this problem, most significantly the breakdown of family and the myth that a support check can replace a father.

But don't underestimate the power of pop culture, particularly when it comes to music.

I think most people will admit that popular music contributed to the free-sex, drug culture of the 1960s. So why not believe that violence-ridden rap music contributes to the rampant black-on-black violence we read about every day in our local newspapers?

I'm embarrassed to admit this, but I am a fan of the culture's music. The culture

Wearing a bright purple suit Tamarick Vanover leaves the Federal Court House after being sentenced

has influenced my dress and speech. I wrote many stories about hip-hop performers when I was a reporter for the Charlotte Observer. I buy the magazines that cover hip-hop music and culture. I was fascinated by the life and times of Tupac Shakur, the most influential and despicable rapper of all time. I even do freelance work for VIBE magazine, a terrific, upscale, watered-down hip-hop mag.

However, I am a fan who realizes hip-hop's harmful side effects.

Hip-hop music has virtually legitimized the drug dealer in

inner-city communities. Through their music and videos, hip-hop artists have glamorized "Ballers" to the point that they're more respected and revered than any working man in some communities.

Hip-hop also is responsible for the proliferation of the black-athlete entourage, often referred to as "my dawgs from the 'hood." A great deal of the time they're nothing more than a collection of uneducated, jobless cousins and childhood friends who play important roles as leaches, flunkies, and nightclub fight-starters.

Hip-hop artists travel in packs. Now, it's almost criminal for a young black professional athlete to roll without a posse. According to ESPN reporter Chris Mortensen, the Baltimore Ravens wanted to talk to Ray Lewis about his unsavory posse of friends. Carruth allegedly plotted a murder with his criminal entourage. Morris' and Vanover's problems seem to stem from hanging with the wrong "posse."

Hip-hop music preaches that young black men who dissociate themselves from childhood friends who have chosen a criminal lifestyle are sellout Uncle Toms. It preaches that "real brothers" do dirt (commit crimes) and are willing to kill or beat down a (N-word) if he's been disrespected.

The ties between hip-hop artists and young black professional athletes are strong. I once attended a party for NBA star Allen Iverson in New York, and it was filled with rappers. Derrick Thomas has many rapper friends. Shaquille O'Neal thinks he's a rapper.

We shouldn't be surprised by the connection. Rappers and jocks are young black men with similar backgrounds and lots of disposable income and free time.

Since the slayings of hip-hop superstars Tupac Shakur and Notorious B.I.G., we're no longer shocked when we hear that a rapper is involved in some type of violence or lawless activity.

From here on out, let's not act shocked when we learn that a hip-hop athlete is involved in criminal activity. It's a big part of the culture that too many young black men have bought into.

■

Magazine attack was low blow
June 15, 1995

*In the 1993 issue of "Dick Vitale's Basketball," writer Joe
Smith included a line insulting KU women's basketball
coach Marian Washington's coaching ability. In October
1994 Washington filed a $10 million defamation suit in U.S.
District Court against Smith, Dick Vitale, the editor-in-chief,
and the publisher. The suit was dismissed in July 1995.
Jason and Vitale have been friends since the days of the Fab
5 at Michigan, but Jason's response to the incident resulted
in a heated phone argument between the two.*

If Kansas women's basketball coach Marian Washington
wins her $10 million lawsuit against Dick Vitale and his
lackeys, it won't be a good sign for yours truly.

Washington, K.U.'s coach for 22 years, is suing Vitale and
the people responsible for publishing and writing a deroga-
tory (and Whitlock-esque) statement about her that appeared
in Vitale's 1993-94 college basketball magazine.

It reads: "The Jayhawks are loaded with talent. But coach
Marian Washington usually finds a way to screw things up.
This season will be no different."

It's obvious the author of that statement, co-defendant Joe
Smith, doesn't have a high opinion of Washington, one of

the pioneers of women's college basketball. And if you've read many of my columns, it's obvious I'm all for stating an opinion — whether it's flattering or unflattering.

That said, I support and understand why Washington is suing Vitale, Smith and several other people involved in the publication of Smith's opinion under Vitale's influential name.

I have no opinion on Washington's coaching ability.

I've seen her team play one time. That was last season when the Jayhawks nearly upended unbeaten and eventual national champion Connecticut in a well-played game. Other than that, I only know her record, which — other than little success in the NCAA tournament — is excellent. (She's a female Norm Stewart.)

I do, however, have an opinion on the publication of Smith's opinion about Washington in a preseason magazine such as Vitale's.

It's gratuitous, sexist and unbelievably unfair.

You can't explain this away by simply saying, "Everyone has a right to an opinion." Or "It's the truth."

If Vitale or Smith want to get into the truth-telling business of journalism, then they must tell the truth (as they see it) on everybody.

I searched nearly all 160 pages of Vitale's magazine, and only on page 137 — in the less than half an inch devoted to Kansas' women — did Vitale's writers find it appropriate to dish out raw, uncensored "truth."

In the 158 pages devoted to men, I searched for nuggets of truth about the high- and low-profile coaches I feel are suspect — Billy Tubbs, Jim Boeheim, Clem Haskins and Lou Henson. Not surprisingly there wasn't a negative word.

The magazine, like most of these magazines, is cowardly.

You see, it's easier to take a shot at a women's coach. Vitale doesn't need to interview Washington, Iowa's Vivian Stringer or Tennessee's Pat Summitt.

But he interviews Bob Knight, John Thompson, Steve Fisher, Dean Smith and almost every other men's coach regularly. That's why in Vitale's magazines you'll never read something like "Bob Knight is one of the smartest men to ever coach basketball. But Knight's teams often under-achieve, because 'The General' is such a jerk, many of his players quit or never develop confidence."

Yeah, I know why Washington is suing Vitale. It's tough enough being a female women's basketball coach without having parents and potential recruits being told by opposing coaches that the most famous man in college basketball thinks you stink.

I'd be sensitive, too. Now that women's college basketball is becoming more popular (and profitable), male coaches are stealing jobs from qualified, deserving women, and male journalists are getting their jollies dissing Washington, one of the people who did all the dirty work that helped make coaching collegiate women so attractive.

If there's justice, Washington's suit will slow them.

■

Magic shows how far athletes go for fanfare
July 5, 1998

In 1998 FOX launched an attempt to muscle in on the late night talk show market. Earvin "Magic" Johnson hosted "The Magic Hour," a short-lived, disaster of a show. Magic may be Jason's favorite pro athlete, but even Jason had to diss "The Tragic Hour."

So I'm perched in front of my television set late Thursday night watching radio shock jock Howard Stern make a fool of Magic Johnson.

And that's when it hit me that under no circumstances should Michael Jordan retire from professional basketball. I don't care if Jerry Krause, the Bulls' vice president of basketball operations, makes Jordan play with Greg Ostertag, Jacque Vaughn, Scot Pollard, Sean Pearson and Greg Gurley next season.

Magic Johnson's post-NBA life is all the evidence I need that Jordan should never retire willingly. He should only get out of the game when he's unable to make any team's 12-man roster. And with the way the NBA keeps expanding, Jordan probably has another 20 years left in him.

I sure wish Johnson would come back out of retirement. He had more dignity as a libido-driven basketball star than as a family man talk-show host.

Stern began "The Magic Hour," Johnson's new late-night gabfest, performing with his sophomoric band, The Losers. The group's performance reached a crescendo when two of its members got down on all fours and passed gas into strategically placed microphones. They did that for what seemed like two hours, but in reality it was less than two minutes.

I was half-offended.

Soon though, as Stern peppered Magic with a litany of insults disguised as questions — including asking Johnson to admit he contracted HIV the fun way — my offense turned into pity for Magic.

By the time Stern groped (and motioned for Magic to grope) the backside of Playboy "Playmate of the Year" Karen McDougal, my jealousy...I mean...outrage had reached a boiling point.

How had Magic Johnson, the original MJ, one of the greatest and classiest athletes of my generation, fallen this far this quickly?

Don't misunderstand. I'm not some prude who doesn't find Stern funny. Stern is a comedic genius. He has mastered the art of viciously and comedically belittling himself and others. No one can match Stern insult for insult.

But why would Johnson invite Stern on his show knowing that Stern was going to flog him in front of a national television audience for 60 minutes? (Stern, Johnson's harshest TV critic, bragged all last week on his radio show that he was going to embarrass Johnson.) Is saving a laughably bad TV show that important to Johnson, who is reputedly worth $100 million to $200 million?

I think it's that important when your drug of choice is public adulation.

A few weeks ago I had this conversation with a couple of

Hollywood celebrity types who were in Kansas City for Derrick Thomas' golf weekend. The consensus seemed to be that athletes and entertainers are all in some way addicted to public adulation and that Magic's addiction is even stronger than the average celebrity's.

That's why he can't walk away from the spotlight. His basketball career ended prematurely. He has retired and unretired as many times as Larry Holmes. Magic tried coaching. And now, tragically, as Stern pointed out, the man who put the EBON in ebonics has hired a speech coach and an interview coach and has launched a late-night talk show.

Seriously, Magic doing a talk show is the equivalent of the late Chris Farley doing an exercise video or Snoop Doggy Dogg heading a campaign to wipe out smoking.

But doing a talk show is a way for Magic to remain in the spotlight. It's a way for him to stand and glow as an audience showers him with applause.

It's my opinion that Jordan shares Magic's addiction; the majority of athletes do. Anyone who has ever experienced the feeling of a crowd chanting his/her name knows there's no greater high.

Jordan would be a fool to walk away from basketball when he's still the best at the game, when he can still move a crowd to shout his name. Jordan shouldn't take that gift for granted. If he does he may retire too soon and spend the rest of his days trying to recapture that glory.

That's nearly impossible to do. Just ask Magic.

Women have to lead charge
July 26, 2002

During the summer of 2002 Allen Iverson was arrested following a domestic dispute with his wife. All but two minor charges were thrown out within a month; as for the other people mentioned by name in this article, Al Unser Jr. voluntarily chose to attend alcohol treatment and Glenn Robinson was sentenced to anger management.

Women shouldn't count on men to combat the rash of domestic-abuse cases haunting high-profile, influential professional athletes. They shouldn't expect David Stern or Paul Tagliabue or Bud Selig to come up with a strong deterrent for domestic violence.

The commissioners can't control their millionaire players any better than the criminal court system can — nor are they terribly interested in doing so.

This is an issue that's going to be closest to the hearts of women, and women almost certainly will find that they are going to have to lead the charge to fight this problem. They can do it — and they should act quickly.

The arrests and accusations continue to pile up. Professional athletes keep getting in trouble for domestic squabbles that turn violent.

Allen Iverson, NBA star, allegedly threw his wife out of the house naked and then tried to hunt her down with a gun. Al Unser Jr., Indy racing champion, allegedly got physical with his girlfriend on a ride home from a strip club and kicked her out of the car.

Glenn Robinson, NBA small forward, allegedly pushed his former fiancee around. In the past two weeks, baseball and football players also have been accused and/or arrested for abusive behavior toward their wives or girlfriends.

There's an obvious problem, and it's not new. And no one thinks this is the exclusive problem of male athletes. Men in all walks of life have struggled with the issue of domestic violence.

What is being debated, particularly among my female sportswriting colleagues, is what professional sports leagues can do to combat a problem that puts players at risk of incarceration and women at risk of injury, as well as damages the image of pro sports. We need to end that debate, because the leagues aren't the ones who will do it.

The men who run these leagues aren't that concerned with the victims of domestic abuse. This is America. We're a self-interested society. Tawanna Iverson isn't David Stern's concern. As commissioner of the NBA, his concern is Allen Iverson and Iverson's ability to attract fans to arenas and televisions.

Plus — and I'm just being totally honest — I think most men don't view domestic violence the way most women do. Men are more likely to see gray areas where a lot of women see the issue in black and white.

Nope. Women will be leaned on to spearhead this charge before others follow. And they have the power to make impact.

Women could do to Allen Iverson what no Pennsylvania court will ever do. No matter what happened between Iverson and his wife, he is going to escape serious criminal prosecution. Police don't have enough evidence, and Iverson's wife, like plenty of abused women, is sticking by her man.

The charges will only enhance Iverson's street rep, which in turn will make him more valuable as a Reebok pitchman.

What if female sportswriters — who, based on my reading, are very upset about the deluge of domestic-violence arrests among athletes — encouraged mothers not to purchase Reebok shoes for their kids until Reebok dropped Iverson as its primary spokesman?

Iverson, regardless of the merit of the latest allegations, has proved to be a poor role model. Mothers could explain to their children why they won't purchase Reebok shoes. This would be a perfect opportunity for a parent to talk with a young boy about the scourge of domestic violence.

Iverson would lose millions. And it would send a powerful message to Iverson's millionaire peers.

■

ESPN goes astray with Rush
October 10, 2003

In an attempt to boost ratings for its NFL pre-game show,
ESPN hired Rush Limbaugh as an analyst for 2003.
On September 28, just the fourth week of the season,
Limbaugh implied that the media gave preferential treat-
ment to Eagles' quarterback Donovan McNabb because
he was black. Limbaugh resigned from the position on
Thursday, Oct 2. Jason himself was called onto the carpet
for a scolding by his ESPN bosses following this piece.

I love ESPN. It's my favorite network. I leave a TV in my basement tuned to ESPN 24 hours day. I watch the early-morning "SportsCenter" reruns over and over again.

ESPN is one of the greatest inventions of my lifetime. Appearing on ESPN's Sunday morning program "The Sports Reporters" is the best perk of my journalism career. I write a weekly column for ESPN.com and make occasional appearances on Jim Rome's TV show, "Rome is Burning."

I love being affiliated in a small way with the true worldwide leader in sports. ESPN is the gold standard in sports coverage.

Sadly, like all great empires, ESPN is spinning out of

control. Drunk on its success and obliteration of CNN/SI, the network has lost track of what made it great — covering sports exhaustively, insightfully and in an entertaining fashion — and is consumed with becoming just like the other networks.

ESPN wants to do game shows and movies and soap operas and give voice to buffoons. Which brings us to Rush Limbaugh.

After claiming on air that Philadelphia quarterback Donovan McNabb is over-hyped because he's black, Limbaugh is right where he and ESPN wanted him to be — at the center of a major controversy. At least, that's what ESPN thought it wanted until this week.

Looking to boost ratings and cover the NFL in a unique way, ESPN added Limbaugh to its NFL pre-game show, "NFL Countdown."

The show didn't need Limbaugh. ESPN already had the best NFL pre-game show in the business. Chris Berman, Tom Jackson, Steve Young, Sterling Sharpe and Chris Mortensen formed the perfect pre-game football family. The group informed, debated, had fun and appeared to genuinely like and respect each other.

The show didn't need an ex-Cowboy just out of rehab, Michael Irvin, or Limbaugh, a political commentator with a right-wing shtick.

But ESPN now always seems to reach for the extreme.

So instead of tweaking a successful show, Irvin was hired to yell and scream, appeal to the Ebonic Nation and make half-baked arguments defending Terrell Owens, and Limbaugh was hired to pretend to speak for the average fan and appeal to the angry, reverse-discrimination white male who is tired of hearing about black coaches getting treated unfairly.

It's been a ratings hit. The numbers are up 10 percent, and that will probably shoot higher as viewers tune in this Sunday to see how the show deals with the Limbaugh controversy following his hasty resignation Wednesday night. I wonder whether ESPN has any idea what it's done to its credibility?

The network that I love already has a brewing problem with NFL players because of its horrid drama series "Playmakers," which relies totally on negative stereotypes about professional athletes. I wore a "Playmakers" hat into the Chiefs locker room after the Baltimore game, and Ryan Sims and Vonnie Holliday both criticized me for wearing it.

Now Donovan McNabb, a popular, likable player, was unfairly blasted on ESPN, and no one on the set defended McNabb from Limbaugh's meritless comments.

McNabb had to waste his Monday news conference responding to accusations made by a political commentator who has never played pro football or covered it as a journalist.

ESPN needs to be careful. The network had found the proper formula for meshing sports and entertainment. Its anchors give you the news with a wonderful dash of personality. "Pardon the Interruption" is a terrific show.

But the network is getting too caught up in inventing the next new sports-entertainment phenomenon. Someone needs to protect the franchise, the bread and butter that made the network a cultural force. There's an art to taking over a ship and keeping it on course. If you keep the right ship on course, it will run over the next pot of gold without anyone looking for it.

Part of me believes ABC, ESPN's big sister network, wanted Limbaugh on "NFL Countdown" as a way to test him out for "Monday Night Football." I once believed Limbaugh could help "MNF." Now that we know better, let's hope Limbaugh slithers back into Bill O'Reilly's shadow.

■

Chapter 6

Yes It's Serious, But That Doesn't Mean You Can't Laugh: Sometimes Sports Are Just Fun

Bring it on: Take notice, all you Texans

March 6, 1997

After hosting the Big 8 Tournament for 20 years, in 1997 Kansas City prepared for the first Big 12 Tournament. To welcome the good people of Texas to our city and prepare longtime Big Eight supporters for a new breed of fan, Jason penned this piece. This was the first barrage in a Whitlock-Texas war that makes the battle between Michael Moore and George Bush look tame.

As you read this, hundreds upon hundreds of Texans are jammed into pickup trucks along I-35 or crammed into Southwest Airlines' flying buses making their way to our fair city.

Lock up your turquoise, get your teen-aged daughters off the street by sundown and pick up Jeff Foxworthy's best-selling audio tape, "Hooked on Hillbilly-onics: Climbing the Texas Corporate Ladder."

It's going to be an interesting weekend.

Yes, the Big 12 Conference's brain trust, the men and women who nurtured the Southwest Conference into greatness and eternal NCAA probation, are on their way to Kansas City to inspect our little basketball tournament.

Kemper Arena, the Blunder Down Under, the Dump with a Hump, has been spruced. New seats, a little dusting and a rearrangement of outside debris has the old girl looking like an abandoned warehouse where livestock and future farmers gather once a year to be spayed and neutered.

Kansas City, it's the first Big 12 men's basketball tournament.

It's important that we put on our best face for the innovative Texas men and women who hope to raise the Big 12 to the level of the gone-but-never-forgotten Southwest Conference.

This is our moment in the spotlight, Kansas City, our chance to show Texans that we're as good as them, our chance to explain to Texans that a "crossover dribble" isn't when hot and mild barbecue sauce stains the front of your shirt.

Not that Texans are illiterate when it comes to basketball.

On the contrary. Texas, Texas Tech, Baylor and Texas A&M have legendary basketball programs. Why the all-time greats at these schools read like a who's who of the NBA 10-day contract.

Terrence Rencher, Sonny Parker, Vernon Smith, Terry Teagle, Slater Martin, Dub Malaise, Rick Bullock are just a few of the names. I mean really, will anyone ever forget Texas Tech's Bubba Jennings' five-year college career?

Compared with these Texas legends the names of Wilt Chamberlain, Danny Manning, Mitch Richmond, Wayman Tisdale, Bob Kurland, Jeff Hornacek, Jo Jo White and Rolando Blackman seem out of place.

We should be honored that our Texas friends have allowed us the privilege of being host to this tournament. Let's all do our part to make Big 12 commissioner Steve Hatchell and his gang feel welcome.

The key to doing that is identifying a Texas visitor from the usual riffraff that descends on us this time of year. This won't be difficult.

Anyone wearing red and yellow, snapping pictures as if they're in Las Vegas and can be heard saying,"This is the best vacation since we went shopping in Des Moines," is an Iowa State fan.

Anyone overheard saying, "You just wait. Norm isn't losing it. Next year we're going to be really good" is a drunken Missouri fan. Approach these people carefully.

And anyone overheard saying, "Let's have drinks in Indianapolis," is a Kansas fan.

The Texas contingent should snap up the remaining 500 tickets. And they'll be easy to spot. Their women wear too much makeup, prefer to wear clothes made by the French designer Cleavage and answer to the name Mary Jo Ellen.

Of course, the men wear 10-gallon hats, belt buckles the size of a cellular phone, answer to the name Billy Ray Joe Bob, and they try to end all sentences with the word "knowwhatImean."

(According to "Hooked on Hillbilly-onics," knowwhat-Imean means: "I don't know what the heck I just said, do you?")

Mayor Cleaver has requested that I warn all casino operators, Westport business owners and self-employed topless models to be extra careful this weekend. Texans cheat, settle bar disputes with shotguns and enjoy videotaping their sexual encounters.

They also know absolutely nothing about playing host to a major basketball event. So I'd suggest they keep their mouths shut, enjoy the barbecue and not interfere with our good time.

■

The club has a spot reserved
September 7, 1995

In an attempt to gain membership into Kansas City's most exclusive club, Jason approached his fictitious friend Dr. B.A. Homer about joining the Kansas City Country Club. This column remains a favorite of Ollie Gates and angered many members of the lily-white golf club.

"Jason, my good friend, come on in," Dr. Brian Anthony Homer said as he greeted me at his office door. "What brings you here? Your next appointment is the day after the Chiefs play at Dallas."

Yes, I know. But I got this letter from you in the mail, and I'm a little confused as to why you would send me this application for the Kansas City Country Club.

"Oh, yes, you got my letter. Good, good," replied Dr. B.A. Homer, Kansas City's leading sports therapist. "I'm a member of the club. I read your comments in The Star about applying out at the club. Well, I know all the right people, so it won't be any problem getting you in."

Doc, there might be some confusion here. You sent me an application for a job as a bus boy.

"I'm sorry. I just assumed. I know how you hate the heat.

I assumed you didn't want to caddie. What kind of work are you looking for? We don't need any help in the kitchen. There might be an opening for a night bartender. Let me call Overland Snobenpark. He and I were just discussing this over a game of bridge."

Wait. Don't call anyone. I've got a job.

"Jason, don't let foolish pride stand in the way. You and I both know it's only a matter of time before The Star comes to its senses and cans your %$&@. You might as well have something to fall back on."

"Listen, we tip our help very well. We've got a young waitress, Laqueesha Kenyawntay, who wears enough gold around her neck and on her teeth that she needs a full-time security guard. I've been meaning to introduce you to Laqueesha."

Doc, stop. I'm not applying for a job. I want to apply for membership.

"Membership?" B.A. Homer said as he took a deep breath and sank deep into his chair. "Membership to what?"

The Kansas City Country Club.

(Silence blanketed the office for several minutes.)

Dr. Homer, are you all right?

"Yes. I'm fine. I was a little lightheaded for a moment. It's from all the excitement the last few days with the Royals and the Chiefs. Now, Jason, run that by me again. You want to join our club?"

Yes. From what I understand, you've got a great course, the people are friendly, and the K.C. Country Club would be a great place for me to meet all the right people. What's the problem?

"Well, Jason, of course you realize ... uh ... how should I say this? Of course you realize we've never had anyone quite like you apply?"

You mean because I'm black?

"No, no, no. Of course not. I mean, well, uh, I mean we've never had anyone quite your size apply."

Hey, Doc, don't try that. I've seen some of the members' wives, including yours.

"Did I say size? I didn't mean to say size. I meant to say someone so wise. And as smart as you are, you can appreciate why our club values tradition, heritage, a family name. My family has been a member of the club since my great-great-great-grandfather Biffington Alexander Homer joined in 1853. Biffington opened Kansas City's first railroad. How did the Whitlocks acquire their wealth?"

My granddaddy, we called him Paw Paw, ran numbers and loan-sharked at the Chrysler automotive plant in Indianapolis. He died when I was just a little kid, and my Uncle John, Paw Paw's oldest son, took over. But really, I don't think the Whitlocks would be considered wealthy.

"I see."

Doc, what do you think my chances are for membership?

"I'd say about as good as Ewing Kauffman's were."

■

Oprah's the perfect match
May 5, 2004

In 2004 Oprah Winfrey launched the "Hi Gorgeous:A Celebration of You" tour. The four-city event made it to Kansas City and the fictitious Dr. Brian Anthony Homer, looking out for Jason's best interests, arranged for a private, intimate meeting.

"Jason, I've found the perfect woman for you," Dr. Brian Anthony Homer told me late Monday night as we began our weekly therapy session. "She's everything that you need. I've arranged for a first date this Saturday night."

Naw, Doc, I'm busy. I've already made plans.

"Change them! This girl is can't-miss. She's a knockout," proclaimed B.A. Homer, Kansas City's leading sports psychologist and therapist. "You're gonna fall in love Saturday night. I guarantee it."

I'm busy. And I've given up on love. I have no luck when it comes to my heart, Doc. You know that.

"Jason, in the 10 years we've chatted, have you ever known me to lie about a woman?" B.A. Homer asked. "Have I ever told you about a perfect woman?"

No. I guess you haven't. Well, there was that entertainer

at your brother's bachelor party. You said she was perfect. What was her name, Mercedes? Or Lexus?

While in Kansas City Oprah asks: "Who thinks I should date Jason Whitlock?" The majority of her fans show their support of the idea.

"It was Destiny, and that's totally irrelevant," B.A. Homer responded defensively. "I'm talking about the perfect woman for you. The woman of your dreams. I'm talking about a woman who is bright, articulate, beautiful, accomplished, classy, worldly, pure and beloved."

Janet Jackson!

"No!"

Latoya!

"Jason, shut up! I'm talking about Oprah. Oprah Winfrey."

Oprah?!?! Oprah is old enough to be my ma... well, she's old enough to be my mama's little sister. She's old enough to be my auntie.

"She's not old. She's mature. She's elegant. She's perfectly aged. She's just what you need. She's positive and free of cynicism."

She's engaged. Steadman. Hello!

"Steadman's not a closer, Jason. Steadman is Mike McDougal with the bases loaded. Steadman has all the tools but he can't get the job done. Oprah's 50 now and looking for a young tiger, a go-getter. She's tired of stringing Steadman along. It's been more than a decade. It's time to move on."

Why me?

"She saw you on ESPN and began asking around about you. She's been reading your column for a couple of years. From what I understand, you're the only reason she's coming to Kansas City. Her 'Hi, Gorgeous' tour is only going to four cities. She chose Kansas City to meet you. I've arranged for a private, romantic dinner at Plaza III late Saturday night."

So she's a sports fan?

"Yes."

What's her take on Jeff George?

"Loves him. Wants to book him on her show so she can help get him back in the NFL."

What'd she think of the Chiefs drafting Kris Wilson in the second round?

"Her sources say that Tony Gonzalez isn't on the trading block, but that Carl Peterson will listen to offers that include a No. 1 receiver and a first-round draft pick."

Hmmm. What does she think the Royals should do with Beltran?

"Pay him. If Sweeney's worth $11 million, then Carlos is worth $20 million. She said, 'David Glass ain't broke, baby.' Oprah has major love for Carlos."

This sounds too good to be true.

"It's not, Jason. You're sitting in the driver's seat to America's real First Lady."

She's just like all the rest. She just wants me for my money and my body. I'm just another conquest, another challenge, another beautiful face for her to toy with.

"You're not taking your medication, are you? You're hallucinating right now. How many fingers am I holding up?"

Get your hands out of my face, Doc. I'm not crazy. You have no idea what it's like to be a sex symbol, for people to ignore your brain and never get past your body.

"Trust me, Jason. She doesn't want your body. Scientists want it for research, but that's about the only people who want to see it. She's interested in you."

I'm not sure it's a fit. She had some critical things to say about the beef industry. Mr. Gates wouldn't like her. She wouldn't really fit in around here.

"Around here? What are you talking about? Oprah lives in Chicago."

Well, she'd have to come here. She'd have to be supportive of my career. I've invested a lot of money in my home. I just laid new tile in my half-bathroom. I'll have a finished basement by next summer. I mean, seriously, I'm not going to just walk away from all of this. I'm not that easy.

"Or smart."

■

Point is, MU down for count
March 21, 1995

Prior to the NCAA second round game between MU and eventual national champion UCLA Jason predicted a blowout win for the Bruins. Following UCLA's narrow escape he received calls from Tiger fans basking in the glory of their near miss. This was Jason's response.

INDIANAPOLIS - "Hey, Mr. Smarty Pants! Mr. Know It All! Mr. Fat Boy!" the voice on the phone yelled at me Monday afternoon. "You owe me an apology."

First off, I'm not fat, I told the caller. I'm handsomely husky. I'm corpulently cute. I'm big-bonedly beautiful. Many have mistaken me for Denzel Washington's younger brother. Second, who's this and how'd you get my number?

"How I got this number is irrelevant. Your apology is the issue. And if you must know, I'm Dr. William Allen Homer, the son of Dr. Brian Anthony Homer. Today, I speak for all Missouri basketball fans everywhere when I say you owe me an apology."

Billy Allen Homer (or B.A. Homer), a longtime Columbia sports therapist and the illegitimate son of Kansas City's Dr. Brian Anthony Homer, was the first of many Tigers basketball fans to call my office Monday morning.

Somehow, Billy managed to get my number in Indiana-polis, where I was recovering from the opening of Michael Jordan's reunion tour.

"You owe all Tigers fans an apology," Billy said. "You and everybody else who said Norm and the boys would get killed by UCLA were wrong. We outplayed them. This is a great day in Missouri basketball history."

Uh, I'm not sure what you're talking about, Billy. I never said UCLA would kill Missouri.

"Mr. Whitlock, please refer to me as Dr. Homer. And I am currently holding Sunday's Kansas City Star sports section, and in it you say that UCLA will beat Missouri by 30."

That should read by 30 one-hundredths of a second. Perhaps there was some computer malfunction or typo-graphical error. I haven't seen the paper. I've been out of town covering the Sweet 16-bound Jayhawks.

And by the way, Billy, while I was in Dayton your brother Brad, Dr. Brad Albert Homer, told me all about how you lost your medical license some years ago during the "Detroit pipeline" investigations.

"That matter is still going through litigation! I will be com-pletely exonerated! Can I help it if Detroit kids thought Columbia was a Motown away from Motown?"

"And there you go again confusing the issue. The issue is how wonderfully the Tigers played against UCLA, the No. 1-ranked team. Sunday afternoon was the shining moment in Missouri tournament history. And you need to recognize that."

A loss in the second round? You've got your chest all stuck out over a close loss in the second round?

"You don't get it. If someone had stopped that little rug rat Tyus Edney, if somehow we don't let him dribble the length of the floor in 4 seconds, we probably would have gone all the way to the Final Four. So in essence we're a Final Four team. Norman Stewart, after more than 20 years, has got the monkey off his back. He finally put together a Final Four team."

What Norm needs to put together is a Final Four Seconds team.

"That was cheap."

I know. But it's hard for me to understand fans who take so much pride in failure. In the last 20 years of Missouri football, the proudest moment was the Colorado fifth-down loss.

"We like to call it the Colorado fifth-down victory," Billy said, his voice quivering. "I'm sorry. I get overcome with emotion when I think of that beautiful day, when we beat the eventual national champions everywhere but on the scoreboard."

Perhaps that's a good motto for Missouri fans: We're No. 1. Everywhere but on the scoreboard.

■

Rivalry requires my help
October 6, 1994

This was Jason's third column for The Star and then-sports editor Dale Bye spent the entire day answering phone calls from irate readers who didn't get the sarcasm. This column sparked the first meeting between Jason and broadcaster Don Fortune as Jason appeared on Fortune's show the day of the game. The column was also referenced by K-State head coach Bill Snyder in his post-game remarks following the Wildcats' victory.

I 'm sure everyone associated with tonight's Kansas State-Kansas football game in Lawrence is a bit nervous.

There's a national television audience via ESPN. A national ranking is at stake. K-State, 3-0, is ranked No. 19. Kansas, 3-1, could crack the top 25 by winning. Both teams have bowl aspirations, the winner tonight being a virtual lock for postseason play. There could be a sellout crowd of more than 50,000 at Memorial Stadium.

This once ho-hum rivalry has blossomed into a pretty big deal. It's the biggest happening in the state of Kansas since Ponderosa added hot wings to its buffet line.

But under the right direction, and this is where I come in, this clash for state supremacy could soon compare to the great rivalries of our time.

K-State vs. KU could compete with such storied rivalries as USC-UCLA, Auburn-Alabama, Miami-Florida State, Notre Dame-Michigan, Ball State-Indiana State, Iran-Iraq and the most celebrated all, John Bobbitt-Lorena Bobbitt.

But, for this to happen, there needs to be a little fine-tuning within each program, and fans, coaches and players must conduct themselves properly.

Here are a few suggestions:

Whatever the weather, the game must be a sellout. The nation's eyes are upon Kansas. If people in this area don't appear to be bonkers over this rivalry, viewers won't take it seriously.

I have little doubt that K-State alums and fans will show up in force. I checked with several local bowling alleys, and many of the Thursday night leagues have been canceled for tonight. To further limit conflict, Manhattan Mayor Roger Maughman shut down his city's bingo halls.

It's you KU fans that trouble me. You must postpone your bridge club meetings, skip Biff's soccer match and pull Christine out of her ballet lesson.

I know football is a barbaric bore, and the money dumped into the program could be better used in KU's academic departments researching crucial areas of science. Like, why doesn't the BMW 325i handle rainy weather as well as the BMW 324i? Or, are there harmful psychological side effects to your 16-year-old child if his/her first car costs less than $16,000?

But let's overlook the financial waste and support the Jayhawks.

Proper attire is vital tonight.

K-State fans, wear your Sunday best — jeans with fewer than two stains and a nice flannel shirt. Male Wildcat fans should wear the same thing.

KU men, no scarfs or sweaters tied around your necks. Have a rugged look. Don't shave and put on a pair of boots. Lady Jayhawks, leave the diamonds and pearls at home. Envious Wildcat fans might try to steal them. You know how peasants are.

Crowd noise is essential. But not just any kind of noise. The truly great rivalries bring out the worst characteristics in otherwise sane human beings. Chants of "Buuulllll Droppings! Buuulllll Droppings!" whenever officials make a call that negatively affects your team will let viewers at home know that this is a passion-filled battle (and that KU fraternities tapped a few kegs before kickoff). It's probably too late for this next suggestion, but the big-time programs tend to have an unseemly side hiding just beneath the surface of their squeaky clean images. K-State's recent spat of drinking-and-driving arrests is a step in the big-time direction. But, if a couple of KU players would bump off a liquor store between now and kickoff, that would give ESPN a neat little angle to promote the game.

I guess that's about it.

Oh, there is one other thing. Great rivalries aren't played on the same night as Seinfeld.

By any definition, here's how to mess with Texas

March 5, 1998

This was Round 2 of Jason vs. the State of Texas. Preparing for the second Big 12 basketball tournament Jason tries to bridge the communication gap between himself and the Texas schools. This column also makes direct reference to Texas head Coach Tom Penders with whom Jason had a running feud.

During the last year I've learned that communication is the key to having a successful relationship with Big 12 basketball fans from Texas.

Around this time a year ago poor communication nearly ruined my relationship with Texans. Some of them took offense to a column I wrote that good-naturedly pointed out their many basketball shortcomings and their over-inflated opinions of themselves.

University of Texas coach Tom Penders, whom some call the greatest coach never to win a game of any significance, blew a gasket and threatened to move the Big 12 Tournament from its rightful Kansas City home to a city in Texas, where the tournament, in the tradition of the Southwest Conference, could be properly ignored by Texans.

Penders was so irate that he went on a national radio program and referred to yours truly as a "400-pound buffalo."

Now there's no reason for there to be bad blood between myself and Texans. We're going to be sharing this basketball tournament for years to come. I want to put last year's hostilities behind us. Let's call it a big misunderstanding, a basketball cultural gap.

In hopes of improving our relationship, I spent the last 12 months learning the nuances of Texas basketball. What I discovered is that Texans have a far different basketball vocabulary than the rest of their Big 12 brethren. This vocabulary difference contributed to my problems with Texans.

Again, communication is the key to a successful relationship. In order to get along, we must be able to understand each other.

Here are the definitions of 25 terms you might hear spoken by Texans over the next few days at Kemper Arena, site of the Big 12 Tournament:

1. Tumbleweed: Name of Tom Penders' hairstyle.

2. Tattoo: Secret nickname Texas players have for Penders.

3. De Plane, De Plane: It's what Penders will shout shortly

after Texas' game tonight against Texas Tech.

4. Get Shorty: It's what Texas basketball fans chant at the end of most games.

5. Shot Clock: A drinking game played with tequila that helps University of Texas fans rationalize Penders' coaching strategy.

6. PTPer: A Texas valet service that specializes in "parking the pickup."

7. Diaper Dandy: A cheerleader who is being groomed to date Cowboys owner Jerry Jones.

8. Three Seconds: The amount of time some Texas Tech basketball players spend in class.

9. Final Four: It's what Texans call the Big 12 Tournament — the final four days of the college basketball season.

10. Elite Eight: The Alamo, Troy Aikman, Emmitt Smith, Lyndon B. Johnson, Hakeem Olajuwon, Roger Staubach, J.R. Ewing and The Death Penalty.

11. Sweet Sixteen: It's what many Texans call their parents.

12. March Madness: The time of year when a stupid basketball tournament interferes with media coverage of spring football.

13. Phi Slama Jama: Academic honor — the equivalent of Summa Cum Laude — for athletes who graduate with 2.0 grade-point averages.

14. Fab Five: A special course load for freshman athletes — 1. Readin' and Writin' 100; 2. Philosophy 187: Tupac Made Easy; 3. Chris Berman Nicknames; 4. Introduction to Art: Cool Tattoos; 5. CBA History.

15. Dribble: Substance on Tony Barone's chin during the second half of games.

16. Blue-Chip Recruit: Any high school player who plays outside of Texas.

17. Assist: When your class valedictorian takes your entrance exam.

18. Sellout Crowd: A road game.

19. Triple Double: The name of the burger that made Oprah Winfrey fear Mad Cow disease.

20. Dipsey-do-dunkeroo: Name of gigantic hairstyle worn by Texas women.

21. The Paint: Line of makeup preferred by Texas women.

22. Traveling: The Texas two-step done to rap music.

23. Finger Roll: What a Texan does when he's out of Kleenex.

24. Big Dance: Party at Michael Irvin's house with self-employed topless models.

25. Weak Bench: Outhouse needs a new piece of plywood.

■

The Secret Correspondence of Paul Hackett

For years the "Parody Picks" columns were a regular feature in The Star. Each week Jason would include a humorous take on an issue in the NFL and would make some tongue in cheek predictions for the week's games. Often times the columns included transcripts of meetings and phone conversations, letters, or scouting reports that "had come into Jason's possession by means best left unsaid." Below are three excerpts from the "Parody Picks," all dealing with former Chiefs' offensive coordinator Paul Hackett. The "Parody Picks" were a favorite of both Chiefs' groundskeeper George Toma and former head coach Marty Schottenheimer.

October 1, 1995

According to my well-placed source within Arrowhead Stadium, upon returning Monday to Kansas City from Cleveland, site of the Chiefs' embarrassing 35-17 defeat, head coach Marty Schottenheimer scolded his offensive coaches.

During a coaches-only meeting, Schottenheimer verbally undressed offensive coordinator Paul Hackett, demanding to know what is wrong with the West Coast offense.

By means best left unstated, I got my hands on a memo

Hackett faxed to Schottenheimer later in the week.

To: Marty Schottenheimer
From: Paul Hackett
Subject: West Coast offense
Date: Sept. 27, 1995

Dear Marty:

First let me start off by saying thank you. Thank you for talking Carl into letting me ride the team plane back to Kansas City from Cleveland. Carl's threat — demanding that I hitchhike back — was an overreaction to a very tough loss. Also, thank you for providing me and my family with a 24-hour security force. Although I'm sure most of the defensive players are joking when they say they're going to hurt me and my family, my wife feels much safer with a SWAT team protecting our home. Marty, again, your class and dignity in these trying times is something I'll never forget. Thank you.

Now, as for your questions regarding problems with the West Coast offense. To be honest, I don't know what the problem is. As you well know, I developed a reputation as an "offensive genius," because I happened to be coaching the quarterbacks in San Francisco (1983-85) at the same time Bill Walsh was the head coach of the 49ers. Those were great days back then. Joe Montana was in his prime. Bill came up with brilliant game plans. And I rode Joe's and Bill's coattails into some great coaching opportunities.

I really appreciate you guys giving me this opportunity after I bombed as head coach at the University of Pittsburgh (1990-92) and as the pass-offense coordinator of the Cowboys (1986-88). Again, thank you.

Now, although I can't explain what's wrong with our offense, I do know how to fix the problem. Secretly, I have talked with some of my friends in the 49ers' organization. The 49ers are willing to pull off a block-buster trade that I think

As Carl Peterson looks on, Paul Hackett talks to the media after announcing he will be leaving the Chiefs for USC.

will really benefit our offense. If we send the 49ers Derrick Thomas, Neil Smith, Dan Saleaumua, Kimble Anders, our starting offensive line and our next five first-round draft picks, they'll send us Jerry Rice.

I think it's a pretty good deal.

Your friend,
Paul Hackett

November 10, 1996

Through a strange quirk of fate, a letter written by Chiefs offensive coordinator Paul Hackett that was intended for Joe Montana got delivered to my home. I accidentally opened it before looking at the name on the envelope. Thought you might find it interesting.

Dear Joe:

Hey, how ya doing, buddy? This is Paul Hackett. In case you've forgotten, we met many years ago in San Francisco. I was your quarterback coach with the 49ers in the early 1980s and later was your offensive coordinator in Kansas City. White guy, balding, about 6-foot-1, 190 pounds, wear glasses. You remember me, right? In San Fran, I was the guy who always made sure you had a fresh ball to toss in warm-ups. I cleaned the dirt out of your cleats. At halftime I'd get your water and tell you how great you were playing. I did pretty much the same thing for you in Kansas City, except they let me sit up in the press box and wear headsets during the game.

Remember? You used to call me "Coach Hack."

Anyway, Joe, I'm writing because I'm having some problems and I could sure use your help.

This play-calling thing has gotten a lot rougher since you

went away. I never really got the hang of it in Dallas or at the University of Pittsburgh. But man, it was a cinch back when you were slinging passes. I don't want to bad-mouth a friend of yours, but hey man, it's tough calling plays for Steve Bono. You never know where he's going to sling it. He's killing our receivers. And he's got all the defensive players mad at me. A couple of weeks ago, Derrick Thomas threatened to kick my you-know-what, and Neil Smith said he'd love to help him.

Today, Reggie White and the Green Bay Packers come to Kansas City. It's a big game. If the offense stinks today, I'm afraid Thomas and Smith might do something rash, something I'll regret.

The game is going to be on national TV. I was wondering if you could watch the game on the tube and if I could call you from time to time during the game and ask you which play I should call? Or, if you're really not too busy, think about flying out here. I'll save you a seat next to me.

Sincerely,
Paul Hackett

P.S. Tell Jennifer I said "Hi." If she doesn't remember me, tell her I'm the guy who used to drop off and pick up your dry cleaning every Thursday.

September 7, 1997

OAKLAND, Calif. - A friend gave me a tour of the Raiders' facilities Friday night. We stumbled across a memo in Raiders owner Al Davis' office that shed quite a bit of light on what's been going on with the Chiefs' offense the last four years.

The friend, who signed a huge free-agent contract with the Raiders in the off-season, asked that I not use his name. He prefers to remain anonymous.

To: Paul Hackett
From: Al Davis
Subject: Operation Hackey Sack
Dear Paul:

Great work last week in Denver! When you emptied the backfield on third and short and let the Broncos know you were going to throw I thought maybe you had gone too far and Marty or Carl would strangle you right on the spot.

But they won't do a thing. Those pictures I sent you will keep those guys in line.

But what about this Sack The Hack campaign? Will that be a problem?

Do you need my help?

As you well know, Operation Hackey Sack is very important to me.

I planted you in Kansas City to ensure that Marcus Allen
never makes it back to the Super Bowl. So far, you've done
excellent work. No one suspects that you're working for
me.

But don't be so risky this week. Give Greg Hill the ball a
few times in the first half.

Right now everyone thinks you're just incompetent. Let's
keep it that way.

Just lose, baby,
Al Davis

The Chiefs Will Go 16-0: Bold Predicitions from the Last Decade...Some of Which Were Accurate

Cornered, Chargers fans fight
January 21, 1995

Super Bowl XXIX featured the high-flying San Francisco 49ers against the AFC champion San Diego Chargers. In the buildup to the game, Jason predicted an absolute blowout by the 49ers and said it wouldn't even be worth watching. Jason's prediction made news all the way out in San Diego. Angered Chargers' fans filled Jason's voice mail, San Diego TV stations interviewed Jason and the wildly popular San Diego radio duo, "Jeff and Jer" made a foolish bet with Jason. If the Chargers lost by more than 15 points, "Jeff and Jer" had to fly Jason to San Diego, put him up in a five-star hotel and kiss each other's rear ends. The outcome: the 49ers raced out to a 42-10 lead and "held on" for a 49-26 triumph. In this column, Jason responds to emotional Chargers' fans before the big game.

PARTS UNKNOWN, AMERICA - I'm in hiding. San Diego Chargers football fans are nuts.

My Tuesday column — the one in which I announced my plan to boycott Super Bowl XXL, uh, XXIX because the Chargers are pathetic- made it to sunny San Diego. Chargers' fans are enraged. My phone line and the sports department's fax line have been jammed.

It seems everyone in San Diego has a suggestion about

what I should do on Super Bowl Sunday instead of watching the 49ers rout the Chargers. Several callers and faxers threatened violence. Others took shots at our lovely city.

Honestly, I was surprised that so many people in a gang-ridden, marijuana-infested, second-rate California city knew how to operate a fax machine.

"You have the nerve to say the Chargers are a disgrace to the AFC. Look at your team, the Chiefs. You have one of the dumbest coaches in the league. Joe Montana is the biggest joke in sports. He couldn't direct his team out of a paper bag, and your defense is the most overrated defense I've ever seen. You and your whole town are a joke, and your women are ugly." Joe

-Hey, say what you want about Marty "I Can't Count To 11" Schottenheimer, Joe Montana and the Chiefs' defense, but I won't allow you to denigrate our women. They may be chunkier than those underfed California blondes, but they're just as cute.

"It's time for you to get your head out of a plow. You are not in Kansas. Dorothy is your only claim to fame. Perhaps jealousy inspires your attack on the Chargers and San Diego. It's hayseeds like you who have inspired the Chargers this season. So go ahead and open your mouth, display your obvious ignorance, your stupidity, your narrow-minded attitude." Anonymous

-We'll claim Dorothy and Toto as our area's most famous residents as long as you claim The Chicken as yours.

"Talk about pathetic. The Chiefs hire two has-beens and they end up costing the Chiefs the season with an interception and a fumble. That's pathetic." Anonymous

-This caller obviously has been reading my columns.

"Us surfing, dope-smoking, long-haired, beachgoing, yogurt-eating, Shamu-loving, hippie Californians are in Miami while you sit on your fanny and watch your herd move from one side of the pasture to the other. Don't be afraid when you hear all the thunder and lightning. It's coming all the way from Miami. It's the world champion San Diego Chargers." Anonymous

-The only loud rumbling I'll hear on Super Bowl Sunday is the sound of Chargers' fans jumping off the bandwagon. It'll start around halftime.

"On SuperCharger Sunday, the Kansas City columnist may want to get together with the rest of the Kansas City Chiefs and plan Joe Montana's retirement party." Anonymous

-Joe's retirement bash will be a four-ring ceremony. Stan Humphries won't have any rings at his.

"I can't believe you have such a prejudiced, one-sided

view of the world of football. I can't believe they actually allow you to write a column and that people read it. We're fun-seeking, intelligent, beautiful people that work on improving our minds and our bodies. I'm embarrassed that I've wasted this much time writing you this note." Mary A No. 1 Charger Fan

-Your time would have been better spent trying to improve your pathetic football team.

■

Willis Should still be talkin' 'bout NFL

January 9, 2003

The 2003 Fiesta Bowl was one of the great college bowl games in memory and featured two great running backs: Willis McGahee of Miami and Maurice Clarett of Ohio State. McGahee, a junior, already planned on foregoing his senior year to enter the NFL draft but a horrendous knee injury raised questions about his status. Clarett was just a freshman and under league rules would have to wait two more years before turning pro. Jason argued that McGahee should still take his shot in the draft and said that Clarett should learn from what happened to his counterpart and start fighting for draft eligibility now. McGahee was taken by the Bills with the 23rd pick in the 2003 draft, and Clarett continued his fight to enter the 2004 draft up until the morning of the event.

Willis McGahee should still turn pro. Maurice Clarett should announce right now that he's applying for the 2004 NFL draft. And Mike Lupica better learn to pick on someone his own size.

I wish these were all my own original ideas. But they're not. I stole the first two from ABC college football analyst Gary Danielson, and the last one is the prevailing sentiment resonating with the folks who saw me outwit Lupica on last Sunday's edition of "The Sports Reporters" when we debated the merits of a college football playoff system.

I chatted with Danielson earlier this week on my radio show. He caught me off guard when he suggested that McGahee should declare for the draft despite the gruesome knee injury he suffered in Miami's loss to Ohio State in the Fiesta Bowl.

After I thought about it and debated it with an NFL GM and an NFL superagent, Danielson's suggestion made a lot of sense.

If McGahee is going to be out of football for a season rehabbing a major injury, why not do it under the guidance and support of an NFL franchise rather than in your spare time between classes? Why sit out and rehab for free when you could get paid a low, six-figures salary for working out ... plus get the benefit of the best medical advice money can buy?

Here's the theory. Doctors have already told McGahee that he's capable of making a full recovery. McGahee is going to play football again. It's just a matter of when. So even if he does collect on the $2.5 million insurance policy he took out two weeks before the Fiesta Bowl, he'll eventually have to pay back the money. Forget about the insurance money.

So what's the most productive way for McGahee to spend his 2003 season? Should he rehab at Miami and return for his fifth season in 2004 and enter the 2005 draft?

Playing football at Miami in 2004 would be silly. It's Tailback University. Edgerrin James, Clinton Portis, Willis McGahee ... hell, the Hurricanes had some kid Gore on their scout team this season who is supposed to be better than McGahee. By 2004, McGahee could be third on the depth chart behind a Heisman Trophy candidate and some five-star freshman recruit.

Should he rehab at Miami and apply for the 2004 draft?

No. That would be a waste of time. Yes, his knee would presumably be healthy and his draft stock would be higher than it will be this year. But he wouldn't be a first-round pick. He wouldn't be a second-round pick. He would still be a high-risk pick. There have been amazing medical advances when it comes to repairing knees. But one knee surgery often begats another knee injury (ask Terrell Davis).

I say McGahee has little to lose and much to gain by declaring for the draft now. A wise GM (someone looking to replace Emmitt Smith) would snag McGahee with a late draft pick, sign him to an incentive-laden contract, place him on injured reserve, ship him off to Phoenix to work with strength guru Dr. Charles Poliquin (David Boston's conditioning coach) and pray.

What I just suggested makes more sense than anything Mike Brown and the Cincinnati Bengals have done on Draft Day in the past decade. I guess that's not saying all that much.

Here's another suggestion: Clarett, Ohio State's freshman running back, might as well hire Johnnie Cochran and start his lawsuit against the NFL now. Given what Clarett and his family witnessed firsthand happening to McGahee, Clarett should go ahead and be the guy who changes the NFL's policy disallowing first and second-year college players from entering the draft.

If Clarett starts the process now, maybe by the end of the 2003 season the path will be clear for him to join the NFL after his sophomore campaign. The NFL's policy won't stand up in court. Hell, the policy probably couldn't withstand one Cochran rap verse.

"If Maurice can run dat thang, then with Urlacher and Lewis he must bang."

Which leads me to my final point, the verbal duel I won over Lupica on "The Sports Reporters." I've been waiting four years for my opportunity to out-talk Lupica on the show. He takes such delight in hammering anyone who dares to disagree with him on a topic. I love Lupica, but he is the definition of the New York Know-It-All, and if you don't stand up to him he'll bully you on the show.

Well, finally on Sunday I got the best of Lupica during an exchange about whether college football needs a playoff system. Lupica, just like most of my peers, believes Division I football needs a playoff. I vehemently disagree, and McGahee's knee injury is my latest piece of evidence that we don't need to do anything to lengthen the college football season.

"Should we extend the season another game or two so McGahee can entertain you, make more money for ABC and risk another knee injury?" I asked Lupica.

Lupica responded by suggesting teams shorten their regular-season schedule to 10 games. There's a better chance of me and Bill Conlin winning over the Bachelorette than the season getting cut. When you reduce your debate opponent to making hopeless suggestions, you know you've won.

You see, the desire for a Division I playoff has nothing to do with what's best for the kids who are playing the game. That's why I don't understand people's passion about the issue. As journalists, even sports journalists, we should save our real passion for issues and injustices that negatively impact the powerless.

Why should we, sports journalists, lead the charge for TV networks to make more money off McGahee, Clarett and Ball State quarterback Andy Roesch?

Here's a vote for K-State as No. 1
July 27, 2003

In 2003 Jason had a vote in the AP college football poll for the first time. To start the season he voted Kansas State as the No. 1 team in the country and predicted a 15-0 season with a national championship. On September 20 the Wildcats were stunned by Marshall 27-20, their first non-conference home loss in 41 games. It was the start of a three-game losing streak that saw the Wildcats fall all the way out of the polls.

No team has a better quarterback/running back tandem than Kansas State — Ell Roberson and Darren Sproles are both legit Heisman Trophy candidates.

No team has a more favorable schedule than Kansas State — the Wildcats don't really leave home until October and play just four authentic road games all season.

No team has a more prepared, single-minded coach than Kansas State — Bill Snyder is inexcusably skipping Big 12 media day, choosing to teleconference in his comments so as not to interrupt his schedule.

No team finished the 2002 season stronger than Kansas State — the Wildcats routed their last five regular-season opponents by a combined score of 253-30 before subduing Arizona State in the Holiday Bowl.

And you know, despite the loss of cornerback Terence Newman and linebacker Terry Pierce, Kansas State is going to play some

Head coach Bill Snyder walks off the field after the Wildcats were shocked by Marshall in 2003.

nasty defense — that's what the Wildcats always do under Snyder.

I bring all of this up because Snyder's Kansas State Wildcats sit atop my Associated Press preseason top 25 ballot. The AP's Doug Tucker hooked me up with this year's Missouri vote. It's the first time I've had the honor of voting in something as prestigious and important as the college football top 25. I'll be playing a small role in determining this season's national champion.

The Wildcats are my pick.

Yeah, I'll get ridiculed as a homer for picking K-State. Snyder is perhaps the most disliked (by the media) coach in America. He's uncooperative, boring and stubborn. Last week I called him for a comment about Chiefs free agent Joe Hall, a former K-Stater. Snyder returned my call three days later.

"Sorry I'm late," he said.

We in the media don't like to wait. We like our coaches talkative and "media savvy." Snyder is neither. He's only concerned with being a football coach. Fine with me.

Yes, I would prefer that Snyder take over Roy Williams' role as the state of Kansas' top ambassador. It would be nice if Snyder would kiss a few babies and play nice with the national and local media (and toughen his non-conference schedule).

But he's not. And it doesn't matter.

He's built the best amateur football team in America. And the way K-State's schedule shakes out, the Wildcats are only going to have to prove it three times — Oct. 4 at Texas, Dec. 6 in the Big 12 championship (at Arrowhead) and Jan. 4 in the national title game in New Orleans.

If the Wildcats bring their "A" game to those three tilts, B's and C's will carry them throughout the rest of the season, and the Wildcats will be ranked No. 1 at the end of the year, too.

I can't see the Wildcats losing one of their nine home games (including a season-opening date at Arrowhead). Missouri will be improved, but not enough to beat K-State on the road. The Wildcats owe Chris Brown-less Colorado a thumping. The Tigers and Buffaloes are the only real threats on K-State's home schedule.

K-State whipped Big 12 road foes Oklahoma State, Iowa State and Nebraska by a combined score of 151-29 last season. The Cowboys, Cyclones and Cornhuskers didn't improve that much during spring ball.

The only problem K-State has is its schedule. Too many games. The Wildcats will have to win 15 games to win their first national title. Even playing a cupcake non-conference schedule it's difficult to imagine the Wildcats staying free of critical injuries. Can little Darren Sproles survive an NFL schedule? Same goes for Roberson, who loves to tuck it and run.

Well, there's no turning back now. I turned in my first ballot last Thursday. Here are a couple of other interesting tidbits about my initial vote:

1. Defending national champion Ohio State is No. 6 on my ballot. The Buckeyes got lucky last year, winning seven games decided by seven points or less. They won't get so lucky this year.

2. Washington and Alabama didn't crack my top 25 because of their off-season coaching turmoil. The Huskies have one of the nation's top QBs, Cody Pickett. He's going to miss Rick Neuheisel.

3. Yeah, I gave Missouri some major love, placing the Tigers No. 20. Brad Smith is the truth, the whole truth and nothing but the truth, so help me Lee Corso.

4. Oregon is my sleeper team. One year after going 11-2, the Ducks bombed in 2002, dropping to 7-6. Mike Bellotti is a solid coach. The Ducks, my No. 19, will rebound despite their difficult schedule, which includes a trip to Mississippi State and visit by Michigan.

5. K-State will meet Miami, my No. 2, for the national championship. The Hurricanes won't miss Ken Dorsey or Willis McGahee.

The Whitlock vote

The preseason AP top 25 will be released in mid-August. Here is Jason Whitlock's ballot:

1. Kansas State; 2. Miami; 3. Oklahoma; 4. Auburn; 5. USC; 6. Ohio State; 7. Georgia; 8. Texas; 9. Pittsburgh; 10. Va. Tech; 11. Michigan; 12. Notre Dame; 13. Tennessee.

14. Maryland; 15. Purdue; 16. NC State; 17. LSU; 18. Florida State; 19. Oregon; 20. Missouri; 21. Virginia; 22. Ole Miss; 23. Minnesota; 24. Washington State; 25. Wisconsin

If NBA calls, go for money
May 2, 1996

JaRon Rush was perhaps the biggest college basketball recruit in Kansas City history. Projected by many as the top player in his class, Rush received national attention throughout his high school career and was considered a candidate to skip college altogether and enter the NBA draft. Rush played only 37 games in two seasons at UCLA, ignored the advice of draft experts and declared for the NBA draft after his sophomore season. He's never played in an NBA game and has battled a drinking problem.

The last thing JaRon Rush needs is some more unsolicited advice.

But I'm going to give Rush, a Pembroke Hill High basketball star who is one of the country's most gifted players, a teeny bit more today.

If in the spring of 1998 — the spring of your senior year of high school - NBA scouts tell you that you will be one of the first 12 players selected in the June draft, turn professional, JaRon.

Just so we're clear, let me say the same thing a few different ways.

Take the money, JaRon. Advance to Reading Railroad and collect $200 for passing Go, JaRon. Tell the pie-in-the-sky crowd to kiss the rear bumper of your new Mercedes, JaRon.

For two days I kept trying to think of reasons why Pennsylvania high school star Kobe Bryant shouldn't have turned professional. I couldn't think of one good reason.

Of course, Bryant isn't physically or mentally ready for the NBA.

But you know what?

There's no guarantee that he'll ever be ready.

So why shouldn't he turn professional right now? Bryant's NBA stock or value may never be higher than it is today. The worst-case scenario for Bryant is that he gets drafted 10th or 11th in June, signs a three-year contract worth $5 million or $6 million, bombs as an NBA player and is out of the league in 1999.

In 1999, Bryant, who scored nearly 1,100 on the SAT, could enroll in just about any college in America as a wealthy, 21-year-old freshman and pursue the degree, the co-ed(s) and the beer of his choice, just like the rich frat boys I admired as a scholarship athlete.

Or, in a worst-worst-case scenario, Bryant could go play basketball overseas for a couple of hundred thousand a year and pursue the runway model(s) and the funny-tasting beer of his choice, just like the semirich, travel-happy U.S. politicians I admire.

In high school JaRon Rush was called the top player in the nation. But once he enrolled at UCLA his career went into a freefall.

Think about it. Bryant would probably be risking more by going to college.

Two years ago around this time, I covered the University of Michigan basketball program when it landed high school player of the year Jerod Ward, a Clinton, Miss., product whom scouting guru Bob Gibbons hailed as the next Glenn Robinson. (Regardless of what you think of Robinson's play this season, remember he signed a $68 million contract.)

Ward, 6 feet 8 with three-point-shooting range, was a can't-miss prospect. He planned to play one year of college ball and turn pro. Well, in two seasons of college play

Ward has scored 191 points in 30 games and has had two knee surgeries.

Out of high school, Ward was every bit the NBA prospect that Bryant is today. Now Ward will be lucky to get drafted after his senior year of college.

JaRon, you still with me?

I'm not against education or downplaying its importance. The education I received in college has served me well and contributed greatly to my happiness.

But when I think about how much more I would have enjoyed the college experience with a couple of million burning in my wallet, well, I just have to be honest.

If you're going to be one of the NBA's first dozen draft picks, you might as well turn professional and get your education later.

The pie-in-the-sky crowd will moan and groan loudly about how you're throwing away your youth by accepting NBA millions. Dangle $50,000 in one of their faces and watch what they'll throw away.

KC kids, read this and leap;
KC foes, read it and weep
April 21, 1998

No matter what happens, one thing Jason will always be remembered for is his ill-fated prediction of the Chiefs for the 1998 season. After going 13-3 and just missing out on beating eventual Super Bowl champs the Broncos, the Chiefs made several high-profile off-season moves and were seen by many as favorites for the upcoming year. Jason went so far as to predict a 16-0 season and a Super Bowl title. The team finished 7-9 and is regarded as the greatest disappointment in franchise history.

OK, I'm coming down from my Chester McGlockton high. The Chiefs aren't going to shut out all of their opponents. Dale Carter and James Hasty won't intercept every pass. Derrick Thomas and Leslie O'Neal won't beat the quarterback to the pocket on every play.

But perfection — a 16-0 regular season — is a real possibility.

I've been saying that to people ever since the Chiefs signed McGlockton, the Notorious D.F.T. (defensive tackle). He loves it when you call him "Big Whoppa."

But everyone looks at me strangely or walks away laughing when I mention 16-0.

Everyone except Thomas, the Chiefs' Pro Bowl pass rusher.

"I'm realistically looking at 16-0," Thomas said Monday. "There's no reason why we can't be 16-0. With this kind of lineup, you've got to look at that. You can't look any other way."

I caught up with Thomas on Monday afternoon at the Lucile H. Bluford Library on 31st and Prospect.

Derrick Thomas, John Browning, and Leslie O'Neal looks on as the 1998 Chiefs suffer a 40-10 loss to New England.

Thomas had handed over a check to the Kansas City Public Library for more than $61,000 to repay the delinquent fines of kids across Kansas City. Thomas plans to raise another $58,000 by selling a limited-edition football that commemorates his 100th NFL sack. Fifty-eight footballs signed by Thomas and Denver quarterback John Elway, whom Thomas sacked for No. 100, will be sold for $1,000 each. The money will be used to buy children's books for the libraries.

D.T. deserves mad props and much love for keeping it real and sprinklin' the Benjis in the hoody (ask your kid to decipher that sentence). He's not the only Chief to give back to the community, but he might be the most consistent giver. Anyway, leave it to a sportswriter such as yours truly to show up at a charity function and start talking football. But the additions of McGlockton, Derrick Alexander and O'Neal have made me fantasize about covering a team that will go down in history.

The Chiefs went 13-3 and had the league's best defense last year despite an inexperienced team and several weaknesses. What should we expect now that the personnel of the team has improved so obviously?

"When you come with most of the talent, you can say we should be 12-4, 11-5," Thomas said. "But when you've got all the talent, there's no reason you can't say 16-0. I know that back in the day the Dolphins said they could win 'em all."

The 1972 Dolphins are the only NFL team to complete the regular season undefeated. They went on and won the Super Bowl, finishing the season 17-0. The 1985 Bears finished the regular season 15-1, losing only to the Dolphins. The Bears also won the Super Bowl.

The Dolphins and the Bears were led by extraordinary defenses. The Chiefs have an extraordinary defense.

"On paper we do," Thomas said. "But paper doesn't mean anything. You have to avoid injury and all that other stuff to end up on top. But if I had to put a defense on paper, it would be ours."

It's a defense so good that McGlockton said he wouldn't be surprised if the Chiefs shut out half of their opponents.

"That's realistic," Thomas said. "(Last season) we went 10 games without giving up a touchdown in the second half."

That was an NFL record. Thomas has another NFL record in mind for this season. He wants to top Mark Gastineau's sack record of 22 in a season.

"You can't look at any other goal than establishing a new mark in the league," Thomas said. "Gastineau's mark has stood for many, many years. When he got it, there were other factors in the game that aren't in the game now. Everybody lined up in the shotgun back then. People used to drop back and throw the ball deep back then. Now, they've gone to the West Coast form of passing, and it's all quick stuff and timing."

"But this lineup we have should even out the playing field."

And could lay out all 16 Chiefs opponents.

■

Bring back Gunther
December 24, 2003

*Even before the Chiefs were ushered out of the playoffs
by the Colts in January 2004, it was well known that
defensive coordinator Greg Robinson would be forced out.
After observing the situation Jason made a shocking proposal: bring back former defensive coordinator and fired
head coach Gunther Cunningham to lead KC's defense.
Early in the off-season the Chiefs did just that, and this
year we will find out if in fact Cunningham is the man
who can repair the Chiefs' porous defense.*

Gunther Cunningham would come back to Kansas City as
defensive coordinator. I truly believe that.

Pay him a million dollars just like Monte Kiffin in Tampa
or Marvin Lewis when he was in Washington. Cunningham is worth $1 million as a defensive coordinator. Yes,
he failed here as a head coach. He was too emotional, too
irrational, too unpredictable. He got promoted past his
level of competence.

But Cunningham has no flaws as a coordinator — where
he served the Chiefs well for four seasons. He's wasting
his time as a linebackers coach for the Tennessee Titans.
Cunningham belongs in control of an NFL defense. He's
the perfect defensive coordinator for the Chiefs.

Dick Vermeil doesn't like to involve himself with the defense. He's an offensive coach. He gives his defensive coordinator total freedom. Gunther could return here as a savior. Cunningham is loyal and in no way would try to undermine Vermeil. Cunningham knows how to be a soldier. And Cunningham's players would tell you that he has a huge heart. Cunningham would forgive Carl Peterson for firing him via the Internet.

Show Gunther the money and he'd take Kansas City's current personnel and mold it into a respectable unit. Add a top draft pick and one high-impact free agent, and Cunningham would field a Super Bowl-caliber defense.

Greg Robinson, KC's current defensive coordinator, can't return next season. I know that Vermeil gave Robinson a vote of confidence Tuesday afternoon. Vermeil said Robinson would be defensive coordinator here as along as Vermeil remained head coach.

That's what a head coach has to say in late December when his team is 12-3 and headed to the playoffs. This isn't the time to throw Robinson overboard. Vermeil is still hoping to get lucky. He's praying that Robinson's defense can create enough turnovers to mask a horrible run defense.

It's probably not going to happen. AFC playoff teams are salivating at the opportunity to face Kansas City's defense. The Chiefs' defense is a leaguewide laughingstock. Despite

KC's gaudy record, the Chiefs are probably the least likely AFC playoff qualifier to make the Super Bowl.

When the Chiefs get bounced from the playoffs, Vermeil will have to rethink his position on Greg Robinson. Vermeil said Tuesday that he doesn't bow to media pressure. He doesn't worry about what fans or sportswriters or talk-show hosts think.

Well, he has to worry about what his players think. And based on what we saw after the Minnesota loss — Eric Hicks and Ryan Sims snapping at each other — Vermeil's players are none too happy with the defensive scheme. Robinson's house isn't in order.

Again, Vermeil gives his defensive coordinator total control. The fact that Robinson's players can't wait for reporters to leave before attacking each other is an indication of just how ragged things have gotten on the defensive side of the football. The chaos reflects on Robinson.

Gunther Cunningham is the perfect solution.

Playing sound run defense starts with an aggressive, hard-line attitude. I don't want to generalize too much, but the reality is that jerks coach defense and intellectuals coach offense. Greg Robinson is cerebral. He's an intellectual. He's a nice guy. He's not overly emotional. He's nothing like the Stoops brothers, the college football defensive masterminds.

Cunningham is a madman, and his defenses reflect Cunningham's anger.

The Chiefs can't stop the run because they're soft. Robinson is soft. I'm not saying Robinson is a bad football coach. He's not. He just doesn't have the temperament to be a top-flight defensive coordinator. Robinson would probably be a far superior head coach than Cunningham.

But if you want to stop the run and go to the Super Bowl, go with Gunther Cunningham. He should be Kansas City's defensive coordinator next year.

■

Chapter 8

In the Moment, Part 1: The Successes, Achievements and Accomplishments of the Last 10 Years

Celebration as good as imagined
November 15, 1998

*On November 14, 1998, Kansas State defeated Nebraska
40-30, their first win over the Cornhuskers in 29 years.
For many K-State fans this is the game that officially
marked the ascension of their program to a national
power. K-State president Jon Wefald was so overjoyed
that he tried to wrap his arms around Jason and share
a celebratory hug.*

MANHATTAN, Kan. - It wasn't the parting of the Red
Sea. But it felt like it.

Grown men and women wept openly, holding each other
as much out of disbelief as joy. Children screamed: "We're
No. 1." Families posed for pictures as if they were over-
looking the Grand Canyon. Kansas State fans tossed tor-
tillas onto the field, anticipating an engagement at the
Tostitos Fiesta Bowl. They rushed Wagner Field three
times, stopping the game twice before its official conclusion. K-State president Jon Wefald stood atop a bench
along the sideline and furiously pumped his fist. This
long-awaited moment appeared to feel as good as
Wefald had imagined.

"Twenty-nine years!" shouted Jordan White, an elated K-
State alum, as some 20,000 fans descended upon the play-

ing field. "Let my people go free!"

"I'm happy. I can assure you of that," said understated coach Bill Snyder, K-State's Moses. "I feel very good about this. I'm humbled by it in all honesty."

After three decades of suffering, K-State fans celebrate their 1998 victory over Nebraska

K-State beat Nebraska 40-30 in football Saturday afternoon, ending 29 years of Cornhusker-induced despair, improving its record to 10-0, clinching a spot in the Big 12 title game against Texas A&M and potentially placing the Wildcats three victories from college football's national championship.

The dregs of the old Big Eight are now kings of the Big 12 mountain.

It was far from the rout some K-State fans anticipated. Five turnovers, eight penalties and a gutty effort by third-string Nebraska quarterback Eric Crouch kept the game from getting out of hand.

But judging from the emotion and the deafening sound that

erupted from KSU Stadium in the game's final dramatic moments, it felt as good as a blowout.

The No. 11 Cornhuskers took a 30-27 lead with 8 minutes, 22 seconds to play. Crouch hit Sheldon Jackson with a 9-yard TD pass. At that point, Nebraska's sea of red appeared to have withstood K-State's strongest challenge in three decades.

But Michael Bishop, K-State's brilliant quarterback/play-maker, engineered a methodical, 80-yard-rebuttal touch-down drive that concluded with his Joe Montana-to-Dwight Clark-esque 11-yard pass to Darnell McDonald in the back of the end zone with 5 minutes, 25 seconds to play.

Bishop scrambled right, threw across his body and hit McDonald right between the numbers. Kansas State led 34-30. The Wildcats' defense took over from there.

Travis Ochs, who got away with an obvious face mask, sacked Crouch on a key fourth-down play. And on Nebraska's last, desperate offensive series, Jeff Kelly scooped up a Crouch fumble, dashed about 20 yards, then vaulted himself the final 3 yards across the goal line.

Game over.

Streak over.

Time for bedlam. Time to tear down a goal post.

The only problem was the goal post wouldn't cooperate. Greased before the game, installed and reinforced two weeks previously, the north end-zone post gave K-State students just as tough a time as their peers did subduing Nebraska. It took nearly an hour.

And with K-State's band locked in formation in the stands, still playing, the goal-post ceremony looked like a scene out of "Titanic."

Nothing about beating Nebraska came easy. The Cornhuskers were the first team all year to move the ball effectively and consistently against K-State's defense. Nebraska led 17-14 at halftime. The Huskers gained 255 yards in the first 30 minutes.

The Wildcats made the mistake of using a little bit of the gimmick defense — no down linemen in front of the guards or center — that Oklahoma State had used successfully against Nebraska earlier in the year. It backfired schematically and mentally.

"It's not our style," Snyder admitted. "It's not what we do. It wasn't for us."

In the second half, K-State lined up, played its traditional defense and stuffed Nebraska's offense. The Cornhuskers gained just 96 yards after the break. They had just one first down in the third quarter.

The Wildcats would have won in a rout had it not been for running back Frank Murphy's costly third-quarter fumble that Ralph Brown picked up and ran 74 yards for a score.

But games as important as these shouldn't come easy.

They should be unforgettable, emotionally draining wars, as this one was.

Final payback: Nick, Kirk now among KU's greats
March 30, 2003

On March 29, 2003, the Jayhawks defeated No. 1 seed Arizona in the West Regional final to advance to their second straight Final Four. The victory and return trip to college basketball's marquee event was the defining moment for a team led by two All-American seniors that gutted out back to back victories over Duke and Arizona. The game also served as payback for a 91-74 loss to the Wildcats earlier in the year at Allen Fieldhouse.

ANAHEIM, Calif. - We're never going to forget Kirk Hinrich and Nick Collison.

Their importance to the Kansas basketball program has now been elevated and cemented, lifted to a status right alongside the all-time greats who have donned Jayhawks uniforms.

You can now say Nick and Kirk in the same sentence with Wilt and Jo Jo and Raef and Paul and Jacque and Danny and Drew.

Kirk and Nick were a part of the recruiting class that helped Roy Williams fall back in love with college basketball. They were influential in Williams' decision to pass on his

dream job at North Carolina. They helped knock the NCAA
Tournament monkey off Williams' back.

And now, by leading the Jayhawks to a second straight
Final Four appearance with back-to-back signature performances, Nick and Kirk have hoisted the Kansas program to
its highest level of prominence in a decade.

On the strength of Hinrich's 28 points and clutch three-
point shooting, the second-seeded Jayhawks throttled West
Regional No. 1 seed Arizona 78-75 inside The Arrowhead
Pond on Saturday afternoon.

"I really felt Kirk would
play his tail off,"
Williams said.

Hinrich's six three-pointers foiled Arizona's
collapsing defensive
attack, which focused
on stopping Collison,
who scored 33 points in
Kansas' semifinal victory
over Duke.

*Nick Collison helps Kirk Hinrich to his feet late
in the Jayhawks 91-74 loss to Arizona in 2003.
Two months later KU knocked off Arizona in the
West Regional final.*

Hinrich also made the
defensive play of the game, blocking Jason Gardner's first
would-be game-tying three-point attempt and getting a hand

in Gardner's face on his second heave as the game clock expired.

"Hinrich stepped up big," Gardner acknowledged. "Every time they needed a bucket he was there."

The Hawks needed Hinrich more than ever on Saturday. He struggled against Duke, scoring just two points. On Saturday Collison couldn't get open for any looks and ran into foul trouble. Arizona's 1-3-1 zone clogged the lane and prevented slasher Keith Langford from getting untracked in the paint. And point guard Aaron Miles eventually fouled out of the game.

At one point the depth-depleted Jayhawks had to play three to four minutes without Miles and Collison. Playing alongside Langford, Jeff Graves, Michael Lee and Bryant Nash, Hinrich was the only real offensive threat in the lineup.

"The other guys get so much strength from Kirk," Williams said.

Graves gave Kansas some needed muscle on Saturday. Playing 32 inspired minutes, Graves made all six of his shots and pulled down 15 rebounds. He looked nothing like the overweight and unmotivated big man who opened the season.

On a day when you thought the Jayhawks would really

miss Wayne Simien, Graves made everyone momentarily forget all about Wayne's injured shoulder and what might have been.

Maybe that's how we will remember the Kirk and Nick era.

With Nick and Kirk, the Jayhawks specialized in overcoming every obstacle.

This year's team wasn't supposed to be able to compensate for the loss of Drew Gooden and Jeff Boschee, KU's dynamic inside-outside duo of a year ago. No way the Hawks could make the Final Four without Simien. The selection committee allegedly put the screws to the Hawks by depriving them of a No. 1 seed and sending them to a stacked West Regional that featured Duke and Arizona.

And let's don't forget about all those Roy Williams rumors. And the lack of depth. And Graves' constant foul trouble.

Something was supposed to stop Kansas from getting to the Final Four. Word just never got to Nick and Kirk.

They never worried. They never seemed bothered. When the Wildcats rallied from a 16-point first-half deficit and Williams blew a gasket on the sideline after an official reversed a no-call, Hinrich never seemed troubled.

He opened the second half more determined. His Jayhawks followed suit and rebuilt their double-digit lead. When the Wildcats rallied again, Hinrich dug a little deeper and his Jayhawks followed his lead.

"Ever since I've played with him," Collison said of Hinrich, "I knew he had more heart and guts than anyone I've ever played with or seen."

Nick and Kirk's Kansas teams will be remembered for playing with more heart and guts than we've seen for quite some time.

Tigers fans quench thirst after long bowl drought
December 28, 1997

Few fans in the country showed the resilience and loyalty that MU football fans displayed following the team's appearance in the 1983 Holiday Bowl. For 14 years Tiger fans waited for another trip to the postseason and in 1997 victories over Texas, Oklahoma State, and Colorado earned them a trip back to the postseason.

SAN DIEGO - Let's just say that San Diego's historic Gaslamp Quarter has survived harsher attacks.

Long-suffering Missouri football fans have yet to fully storm the quarter, a picturesque, downtown confluence of shops, brew pubs and dance clubs. The colors black and gold have not overtaken this city, the site of the Holiday Bowl, which pits Missouri against Colorado State at 7 p.m. Monday, the way, say, Kansas State's purple and white overran Dallas a year ago.

"The problem with Missouri," said Dan Debers, a 1995 MU grad, "is that we don't know how to do this just yet. It's been so long since we've done this."

Missouri hearts ached 14 years for this, the Tigers in a bowl game. Now that it's here, only about 10,000 Missouri faithful will drink in the joy first-hand. The trek to San Diego was a bit too far and a bit too expensive for many of the Tigers fans who would love to be here.

Those who are here seem committed to having a good enough time for themselves and those who couldn't make it.

"I love San Diego," shouted Amber Wisneski, 23, a fifth-year Missouri senior, who was among a group of about 25 Tigers fans crammed into the Gaslamp's Moose McGilly-cuddy's early Saturday morning. "The weather is great, the shopping is fabulous, and the partying is awesome."

"I've been waiting five years to do this," continued

Wisneski, holding her fourth Bud Lite. "I wouldn't have missed this for anything."

That sentiment is the essence of the often-criticized college bowl season. Too many bowls, you say? Tell that to the Missouri fans partying like it's 1999 in San Diego.

It would be hard to convince the Tigers fans who are here that the Holiday Bowl isn't as important as the Fiesta or Orange bowls.

It's definitely more than a good enough excuse to stick out your chest and show a little school pride, something Missouri fans waited to do through 14 straight losing seasons.

"Misery. That's been our name for Missouri for too long," said Debers, who flew to San Diego with 11 of his best friends and hung out at McGillycuddy's until 1 a.m. Saturday.

"Man, I never thought this day would get here. We bought our tickets a month ago, the first day we knew we were playing here."

And since then, Todd Coleman, MU's assistant vice chancellor of development and alumni relations, has been planning activities for MU alums. The biggest function should be today, when the Tigers will hold a pep rally at the Hyatt

Regency, the team hotel. Coleman expects 4,000 to 5,000 fans to fill the Hyatt. On Monday, Gov. Mel Carnahan will be the guest of honor at a tailgate party before the game at Qualcomm Stadium.

"We're pleased with our support," Coleman said. "By the time the weekend is over, we'll paint this area black and gold. We've already established Moose McGillycuddy's as the official hangout for Missouri fans. We've got six or seven chartered planes coming in (Saturday). We'll claim the rest of the Gaslamp area."

If they don't, MU fans will be satisfied with a victory Monday night. Colorado State, 10-2 and ranked 18th, averages nearly 37 points a game. The experts are predicting a shootout. Missouri fans, of course, are predicting a romp. "If (fullback) Ernest Blackwell gets the ball 15 times, we'll win by two TDs," said Brandon McManamy, 25, a Kansas City resident and recent MU grad.

"We'll win," Wisneski said while gyrating to a Heavy D rap tune. "We have to. We've waited too long to be disappointed."

Hall-elujah! No team can handle his heat
October 6, 2003

The first half of the 2003 season was magical for the Kansas City Chiefs, and for return man Dante Hall in particular. Hall returned kicks for touchdowns in three straight games and electrified fans across the country in the month of September. On October 5th the Chiefs hosted the Broncos and were struggling to maintain their perfect record, trailing by six in the fourth quarter. Hall then unleashed what is probably the greatest punt return in NFL history.

K ansas City's "Lil Inferno" continued to blaze Sunday afternoon inside Arrowhead Stadium, incinerating the arrogant Denver Broncos, igniting 79,000 rabid fans and fanning the 5-0 Chiefs' Super Bowl flames.

Dante Hall is hotter than your grandmama's fried-fish grease, and subsequently so are his Kansas City Chiefs, 24-23 winners over the previously undefeated Broncos.

The Lil Inferno torched the Broncos the same way he burned the Steelers, Texans and Ravens in consecutive weeks, searing and singeing his way around and past 11 coverage men on his way to a game-extinguishing touchdown.

Kansas City's opponents had better toss away those gasoline

game plans that call for their kickers to boot the ball in Hall's direction. Dante's inferno is blazing out of control.

His fourth-quarter, 93-yard, backdraft punt return befuddled the Broncos. It rescued the Chiefs from the beating the Broncos seemingly were handing KC and made eye-witnesses shiver in disbelief and ponder the history we were fortunate to see.

"I'm still in awe," Chiefs fullback Tony Richardson said more than one hour after Hall's return erased a 23-17 deficit. "That's the kind of stuff you see in video games. That's playground stuff."

With a little more than 8 minutes to play and the Chiefs' offense help-lessly stuck in neutral, Hall fielded Micah Knorr's punt at the Kansas City 7. A herd

Dante Hall weaves his way through the Broncos at the start of his electrifying 93-yard punt return.

of unblocked Donkeys thundered toward KC's 5-foot-8, 185-pound, record-setting returner.

"We didn't block anybody," said Chiefs tight end Billy

Baber. "We were trying to block the punt."

Denver "gunner" Chris Cole, who predicted that the Broncos would shut down Hall, was the first Donkey to arrive on the scene. Hall juked Cole and darted right in the direction of three more Donkeys. Hall then began backing up and reversing to his left, where he avoided Cole again but withdrew all the way inside his 3.

"That was a Bobo move," Hall said, referring to the clown and his backpedal. "They tell me to be smart. The first part of the return wasn't smart. I retreated back to the 5 and then the 2. I got dumber and dumber and dumber."

And then Hall had an idea: "Oh, I got to get out of this jam."

He motored way left, found a posse of escorts — including linebacker Mike Maslowski burying Knorr into the ground — and jogged the last 20 yards into the end zone. It sounds so easy now, but it was truly magical, one of the most electric moments in NFL history.

"He disappeared and then re-appeared," Chiefs running back Priest Holmes said of Hall.

By the time his teammates caught him to celebrate, Hall owned two NFL records — touchdown returns in four consecutive games and four touchdown returns in one season — and the early lead in the race to be league MVP.

"Right now I'd be hard-pressed to find someone who is more valuable to his team than what he is," Denver tight end Shannon Sharpe said. "If they had to vote today, he'd win hands-down. He's as good as I've seen in 14 years of being in the league. I'm talking Eric Metcalf, Mel Gray, Brian Mitchell or whoever."

Hall's 206 return yards trumped Denver's sizable offensive-yards advantage (469-261).

"I'm not going to say we gave it away, because they had something to do with it," Sharpe said. "But it's kind of hard to stomach losing when you gain 500 yards and your offense doesn't turn the ball over."

The Lil Inferno makes statistical analysis pointless. You can't predict when he'll burst into flames or what will set him off. His unscripted return style defies coverage lanes. "The Mastermind," Denver coach Mike Shanahan, all but said there's no extinguishing Dante's inferno.

"Where you going to kick it?" Shanahan replied when reporters asked about kicking away from Hall.

Something like this — Hall's incredible streak — you just have to let it run its course. You can't stop it. It reminds me of Tiger Woods' Tiger Slam, Michael Jordan's three-point barrage against Portland, Reggie Jackson's back-to-back-to-back home runs in the World Series.

Don't try to understand it. Don't worry about what the Chiefs will do when the fire is inevitably doused and Trent Green is forced to make plays in the clutch. Just enjoy it. We're witnessing something special, something we'll cherish 30 years from now.

■

Don't save a seat on bandwagon
April 13, 2003

After a decade of failure the Royals began the 2003 season with the best start in franchise history. While most of Kansas City was caught up in the excitement and wondering how far the upstart team could make it, Jason took a different tack that caught the attention of ESPN's SportsCenter...

If the Royals lose today against the Cleveland Indians, call my boss, Mike Fannin, and complain. His number is (816) 234-4345. He gets into the office around 10:30 a.m. and rarely leaves before 8 or 9 p.m.

It's Mike's fault if the Royals' winning streak ends today. He demanded that I write a column about the Royals.

I was committed to keeping my own record streak alive. By my count, I've written 23 consecutive columns detailing the greatness of Roy Williams, the stupidity of Al Bohl and all the reasons Roy should continue not giving a (rip) about North Carolina.

When I told Fannin that I wanted to pen a column telling Roy that it would be devastating that my unborn children would never get the chance to see him coach at Allen Fieldhouse, Fannin insisted that I switch topics.

"Big fella, Roy knows you love him. We all know how you feel about Roy," Fannin told me. "You write one more column begging Roy to stay and there are going to be rumors."

What Fannin didn't understand is that the Williams debacle had given me the perfect excuse to avoid jumping on the Royals' bandwagon. I could enjoy the Royals' incredible start, which has now reached 9-0, without jinxing Tony Pena's squad. I had pledged to friend and baseball junkie Steven St. John that I wouldn't write a column about the Royals until they lost.

My friends believe the surest way to wreck a bandwagon is for me to hop aboard. Steven contends that if I would denounce Jeff George, my favorite QB, George would win a Super Bowl title within a year.

Fannin refused to back off.

"It would be gross negligence for you to avoid this start, Jason," Fannin said. "Besides, you've been sipping your wheatgrass and exercising, you're losing weight. The young pitching arms powering this bandwagon can hold you."

So we reached a compromise. I'm not going to write anything positive about the Royals until they lose.

I will write this column, but I will not get on the Royals bandwagon. Their hot start is a fluke. They will be the first team in baseball history to start the season 9-0 and lose 100 games. The Royals don't have a legitimate leadoff hitter, batters will begin to figure out KC's young pitchers, Oakland GM Billy Beane will hoodwink and bamboozle Allard Baird into a trade that will send this team into a tailspin.

You like that?

There will be no mention in my column that this is the Kansas City sports team that can finally make my 16-0 prediction come true. There will be no mention in this column that I stood out on the Velvet Dog patio Friday night and shouted down my friend, Scott Cruce, who claimed the

Royals are capable of a catastrophic losing streak.

"That's not possible!" I was allegedly overheard scream-ing. "These young pitchers are too talented to go six or seven games without a victory. The Yankees couldn't walk through Runelvys Hernandez, Jeremy Affeldt, Miguel Asencio, Chris George and the "Ben Franklin Boyz" in the bullpen (they all throw close to a hundred) without getting handcuffed at least once.

I categorically deny making those statements. I was in bed by 9 p.m. Friday and have no recollection of a beautiful young lady sweet-talking me into promising her concert tickets. Didn't happen. And if it did, I can't be held accountable because I was awash in the euphoria of yet another Royals' victory.

Look, I'd love to tell you how significant Saturday's 5-2 victory over the Indians was. George, KC's No. 4 pitcher, beat C.C. Sabathia, the ace of Cleveland's staff.

But I can't do it. This hot start is a fluke. It's against the same weak competition the Royals will face all season. Oops. I didn't mean to point that out. I don't want people drawing comparisons between this year's Kansas City squad and the Minnesota team that shocked baseball last season by dominating weak American League Central opponents.

Yep, I better shut this column down before I mention that the Royals have won all these games without the player some consider the most talented in baseball, center fielder Carlos Beltran.

The Royals stink. Roy, please stay.

■

"I'm staying"
July 7, 2000

In the summer of 2000 Kansas basketball fans endured one of the most apprehensive weeks in Jayhawk history. Following the departure of Bill Guthridge, North Carolina offered Roy Williams the Tar Heels' head-coaching position. Williams asked for a week to make up his mind, fed Jason doughnuts inside Allen Fieldhouse and then announced to thousands of fans at the football stadium that he would be staying at KU.

LAWRENCE - Finally, a happy ending. Unlike the NCAA and the Big 12 headquarters, unlike the Scouts and the Kings, unlike the Chiefs in the playoffs, Kansas basketball coach Roy Williams stayed put and gave us a happy ending.

The University of North Carolina made Roy Williams an offer that many Carolinians thought he couldn't refuse.

A chance to come home. A chance to guide Dean Smith's storied North Carolina basketball program. A chance to fulfill a lifelong dream.

They thought they'd offered Coach Roy a little piece of heaven.

By ending a bizarre week of endless, irresponsible media speculation with a thanks-but-no-thanks telephone conversation with his mentor, Dean Smith, Roy Williams let Carolinians and the rest of the college basketball world know that he already has a big piece of heaven here in the heartland.

Take that, North Carolina.

And take that, NCAA and Big 12 officials, and anybody else who somehow reached the wrong conclusion that this area is a farm system to be pilfered, mined and hoodwinked out of its sports resources.

We own Roy Williams for life. He's all ours. He's more

Kansan than Carolinian now.

"I'm staying," Williams exclaimed Thursday night at a news conference at Memorial Stadium that was attended by more than 16,000 Jayhawks fans who watched on a Jumbotron. "The University of Kansas is where I'm supposed to be."

Take that, Tar Heels.

"I couldn't leave my players," Williams added, summing up his one and only reason for spurning his alma mater's bid to bring him home. "My players became more important than my dream of coaching at North Carolina."

There will be no more questions about Williams going home.

Home is Lawrence. Home is Allen Fieldhouse. Home is where Phog Allen coached and Wilt Chamberlain played and Danny Manning dominated and Richard Scott overachieved and Jacque Vaughn studied and Scot Pollard painted his nails and Raef LaFrentz starred and Nick Bradford matured.

And what a happy home it should be. With this shadow permanently lifted, Coach Roy should take the Jayhawks to new heights. After he gets over the emotional turmoil of telling his Carolina family no, I fully expect Williams to be re-energized in his quest for a national championship. "It should give us a huge bump in recruiting," said KU athletic director Bob Frederick, who sat beaming next to Williams at the news conference.

Williams has been pursuing a national title for 12 years. He'll get it within the next three years. He's too good to be denied. And now, he'll be too focused and too comfortable to be denied.

This is a day to celebrate.

We were counted out from the beginning.

As soon as Bill Guthridge stepped down, Carolina arrogance swept the college basketball landscape. The Associated Press reported that Williams already had cut a deal with Carolina. Dick Vitale immediately started running his mouth about how Roy wouldn't be able to tell Dean Smith no. ESPN's Digger Phelps rattled off a list of potential successors at Kansas.

No one wanted to listen to Williams, a man who doesn't lie. Williams said be patient. He asked for time. He said he was struggling with the decision. He had been on record for years that Allen Fieldhouse was the best place to play and coach basketball.

"You guys can accuse me of a lot of things," Williams said

Thursday, "but no one can accuse me of being a phony."
And no one can accuse Frederick of being a phony, either.
Frederick, who spotted Williams' talent 12 years ago when
Williams was an assistant at UNC, kept telling us he felt
good about his chances of retaining Williams. Frederick
kept saying he felt confident.

But we doubted. Unfortunately, too many of us have grown
comfortable with the notion that there are a thousand
places better than here. We bought into the hype.

North Carolina has more tradition. Take away Michael
Jordan's NBA career and no one makes this argument.
The ACC is a far superior conference. The Big 12 has
more depth than the ACC and, in my estimation, will
surpass the ACC in the next two years.

The beaches and the weather make the Carolinas better
than here. I lived in the Carolinas. The weather is great.
But trust me, you don't want your kids anywhere near a
Carolina school system.

We have so many reasons to be proud of this area. We
don't have to take a back seat to anyone. Just ask Roy
Williams.

Chiefs legends make their Hall mark: Allen yards ahead in intelligence

January 26, 2003

After spending five seasons with Chiefs, Marcus Allen retired after the 1997 season. At the time of his retirement his 123 career rushing touchdowns were the most ever. Five years later, the first year he was eligible for induction, Marcus Allen was voted into the Pro Football Hall of Fame.

SAN DIEGO - Marcus Allen's greatness is no longer in question. On Saturday it was announced that he'll be the only first-ballot inductee in the 2003 Pro Football Hall of Fame class. Allen's legacy, however, is still being debated.

Is he the greatest short-yardage back of all time?

"I hate that label," Allen told a gathering of media and well-wishers at the news conference for the announcement of the 2003 class. "I appreciate it, but I hate it. I felt I was a complete football player. I'm one of the greatest all-round backs."

Will Allen be remembered as a Los Angeles Raider or a Kansas City Chief?

"I'd like to represent both teams, if that's possible," said Allen, who left the Raiders after 11 seasons and a two-year, mysterious spat with Al Davis. "It would be virtually impossible to ignore all the great things that happened when I was a Raider."

We have until Aug. 3, enshrinement day, to figure out Allen's legacy as a runner. As for how he'll be remembered, the Chiefs, Allen's squad for five seasons, have a decided advantage over the Raiders.

Davis is still mad at Allen. Despite the fact that Raider great Kenny "The Snake" Stabler was a finalist for induction, Davis, realizing Allen was a virtual lock, skipped Saturday's news conference.

Chiefs owner Lamar Hunt was there to personally congratulate Allen and field questions about former coach Hank Stram's enshrinement.

Also, Chiefs fans can take satisfaction in the fact that when the 2003 class was announced

Marcus Allen poses with his Hall of Fame bust on August 2, 2003, the day he was enshrined in Canton.

and poster-sized football cards were placed in front of the dais representing the inductees — Allen, Stram, defensive end Elvin Bethea, wide receiver James Lofton and guard Joe DeLamielleure — Allen was pictured in a Chiefs uniform.

And let's not forget that the Hall of Fame game this year in Canton, Ohio, will pit the Chiefs against the Packers. With Stram and Allen going into the Hall, and the Chiefs playing, the enshrinement ceremony will have a definite Arrowhead East feel.

Marcus may want to represent both organizations. But we all know which organization and which fan base will represent Marcus Allen in Canton. Yes, Allen won a Super Bowl, a Super Bowl MVP and a league MVP award wearing silver and black, but Allen is a Chief for life.

As for how Allen will be remembered as a runner? I don't like the short-yardage label or the all-round label. Both labels are true.

On fourth-and-1, there has never been a better running back than Allen. He was automatic. Tall and lanky, looking more like an NFL quarterback than runner, Allen somehow bulldozed and slithered for the had-to-have yard more proficiently than the bigger backs of his era.

And a quick check of Allen's statistical resume reveals his

all-round skills. He was the first back in league history to rush for more than 10,000 yards and catch passes for more than 5,000. A fullback for two years at USC, Allen blocked in pass protection as well as any NFL fullback. He also ran the deep pass routes. Allen was a slower version of Marshall Faulk. But he wasn't as good as Faulk. That's why I don't like the all-round label.

To me, Allen was the most intelligent runner in league history. His savvy kept him healthy for 16 seasons. His savvy and preparation compensated for his lack of blazing speed. His savvy helped him survive his nasty battle with Al Davis. His savvy made him the on- and off-field leader in two different organizations filled with strong personalities.

Allen's teammates, who included Howie Long, Joe Montana, Mike Haynes, Derrick Thomas, Neil Smith, Art Shell and Lester Hayes, couldn't help but respect his football and social intellect.

"I'm proud of the fact I remained a leader with the Raiders even though things weren't going well for me," Allen told me as he walked along the San Diego bay to the Hyatt Hotel for a paid appearance.

Allen said his father, Harold Allen, will introduce him at the enshrinement ceremony.

"Coaches are important," Allen said. "But nobody was more important in my life than my dad. I want everybody to know how important my dad was and still is in my life."

■

Chapter 9

It Doesn't Always Stay on the Field: Race, Gender, and Politics in the World of Sport

NOW is NOT the time
September 5, 2002

This was Jason's first column for ESPN.com's Page 2, a website devoted to opinions that feature many of ESPN's top personalities and columnists as well as guest features by prominent names throughout the world of sports. As Martha Burk prepared what turned out to be a disastrous protest of the Masters, Jason offered a provocative discussion of the differences between racism and sexism.

Earning the "privilege" to smoke fine cigars, exchange dirty jokes and lie about your golf game, sexual exploits and how hard you worked to inherit your wealth with a group of mostly old white men isn't part of the cure for gender discrimination.

Martha Burk and the National Council of Women's Organizations, are you reading?

Augusta National Golf Club, the home of The Masters, the chosen playground for Hootie (Johnson) & His Blowhards, isn't the proper battleground for the war on gender discrimination. It's the equivalent of President Bush sending ground troops to Dallas looking for Osama bin Laden. A hunt for bin Laden in Texas would draw a lot of attention to a very serious problem, and there are a lot of good ol' boys in Texas who could use a swift kick in the ass, but in the end the hunt wouldn't get us any closer to tracking down Osama.

What Burk and her sympathizers must come to understand is that, just like cancer, there are different forms of discrimination and each strand of cancer (discrimination) has a uniquely different cure.

Martha Burk's protest of the Masters may have been a flop but she still remains active in sports. Here she is attending a Title IX symposium in Kansas City during the summer of 2003.

Racial discrimination and gender discrimination are not the same. The side effects, the consequences, the complications are different. Racial discrimination sentences black men to death row at an alarming rate. Gender discrimination prevents women from getting equal pay for equal work. Racial discrimination allows the police to profile and beat black and Latino men without fear of repercussions. Gender discrimination allows pop culture to make massive profits promoting women as sexual objects.

It's foolish to debate which form of cancer (discrimination) is worse (although racial discrimination ravages the entire body). Any discrimination kills humanity.

But it's not silly to discuss what's the best way to go about curing the different forms of discrimination. As a black man, I've grown tired of every group that's discriminated against pointing to discrimination cures used by black people as justification for their actions. When it suits their purpose, gay activists claim they want the same treatment as black people. Funny how they never ask for it when they're standing in court or applying for a bank loan or buying a new car.

This hypocrisy bothers me because every time someone inappropriately uses a platform built to combat discrimination, the gleeful benefactors of that discrimination point to its inappropriate use as an example of why the platform must be torn down.

Which brings me back to Martha Burk and the National Council of Women's Organizations.

They're arguing that Augusta National needs to open its membership to women primarily for the same reason it welcomed a black member in 1990, for the same reason major corporations turned against exclusionary Shoal Creek.

"Do they have different standards for sexual discrimination versus racial discrimination?" Burk has asked. "Do the practices and policies on sex and race discrimination differ?"

Hell, yeah.

Are the consequences different? Hasn't it been proven
in this country that there are benefits to gender-exclusive
organizations and clubs? Women-only health spas populate
our rich suburbs. High-priced, all-girls schools produce
some of this country's finest leaders. Men and women need
places to socialize and develop away from each other. It's
in the best interest of both sexes. We're an overwhelmingly
heterosexual society. Men and women here traditionally
don't isolate themselves from each other the way different
racial and ethnic groups do. Men and women sleep together, eat together, vacation together, carpool together, work
together, go to school together. Men and women, generally
speaking, learn about each other and are given ample
opportunity to develop a healthy respect for one another.

Oftentimes, that's not the case when it comes to race.
That's why racial-exclusionary policies, especially those
established by the majority (power) community, must be
eliminated from our society. That's why black people wanted Augusta National and the nation's other elite golf clubs
integrated. Black people are fearful when the power struc-
ture congregates without anyone representing us. We don't
want to play dominoes or "Pass The Courvoisier" with
Hootie & His Blowhards. Screw them. They think Busta
Rhymes is an old Oklahoma running back. We just don't
want powerful people who never take the time to get to
know us gathering together and making decisions that could

impact our lives. The best way we know how to combat that problem is by sending in a token or two.

Hell, it's not like we slap a pair of knickers and a cardigan sweater on Al Sharpton and plop him on the 18th green. We don't even send a double agent, a Bryant Gumbel. We're more than happy if every Augusta Shoal Geek Golf Club had a couple of Uncle (Clarence) Thomases. We're not trying to make Hootie & His Blowhards uncomfortable. They have a constitutional right to assemble, regale each other with politically incorrect jokes and bitch about the money NBA players make. What's the use of being rich and bigoted, if you can't have a little harmless fun?

Now, I don't want to be totally one-sided. Ms. Burk is responsible for the elimination of all TV commercials during the 12 hours of CBS's coverage of The Masters. For that, every man in America should be thankful.

Women should not be flying high
April 1, 2004

Another favorite from the ESPN.com Page 2 archives. At the 2004 McDonald's High School All-America festivities Candace Parker of Naperville Central High School in suburban Chicago won the slam-dunk contest. Her "accomplishment" was championed by many around the country as a breakthrough for women's sports but Jason disagreed. This column provoked a rebuttal from Parker's brother that even Jason had to admit was well argued. Parker is currently a freshman at Tennessee.

I apologize for being the voice of reason here, but this sports fan has almost zero interest in seeing women dunk a basketball. It's a nice little novelty act that has a very short life span.

In fact, female slam-dunking as a spectator sport died this week when Candace Parker won the McDonald's All-American slam-dunk contest.

Yes, I'm well aware that the PC crowd — and the men and women who measure gender equality by women's ability to become more like men — hailed Parker's victory as a giant leap forward for womankind. ESPN.com even led its site with a photo of her dunking.

It was just another leap backward.

No disrespect to Ms. Parker, but she was handed the title. Her dunks were unspectacular. She won because the boys in the contest failed to complete their dunks.

Her participation, in fact, undermined the credibility of the contest. Why take it seriously? The people running the all-star game didn't. Eventually, neither did the judges.

Hey, I don't want to sound as intolerant as Vijay Singh. But this is different than Annika Sorenstam visiting the PGA Tour. Sorenstam has the necessary skill to compete with the men on the PGA Tour. Parker has almost none of the skills it takes to compete with boys her age in a dunk contest. I'd rather see Parker compete in the men's game than the dunk contest. She'd have a better chance competing in a game than a dunk contest.

Seriously, Parker dunked as well as an old Larry Bird — when he had a bad back.

I realize that Parker was being used to drive interest in the event. I realize that sports — even high school sports — are nothing more than a vehicle to drive TV ratings. It's all entertainment. I was just disappointed with the unrealistic news coverage of Parker's victory. It was condescending and patronizing.

Her pedestrian dunks didn't advance equality or women's basketball. The judges and the crowd treated her like she'd performed with a disability. Seven judges gave her a perfect 10 on her final dunk. Had a healthy boy completed the same dunks in an all-star dunk contest, he might've been booed off the court.

Is that the equality we're looking for?

Parker is one of the most talented female athletes in the world. She's worked as hard as any boy to hone her skills. So it means little when she wins a contest tilted in her favor. That's degrading. And so is the subsequent patronizing news coverage.

The story could've been told straight. No one had to pretend that this was some sort of historic moment in sport. But that's not what we do when it comes to women's sports. We overhype everything. We create monumental myths. There are people who still believe that Brandi Chastain and the U.S. women's World Cup team pulled off the equivalent of the Miracle on Ice.

That's because there's a strong, militant and active segment of our population that too often measures women by the same standards as men. And who says that's a good thing?

Think about it. Men's basketball has overdosed on the slam dunk. American players don't have fundamentals because, among other reasons, they spend too much time working on dunks. There are many people who would argue that the dunk has been slowly killing American basketball.

But we see the dunk as an advance for the women's game. Why? Because some women — in the name of equality — are dead set on doing every dumb thing we do. The women's game shouldn't be played above the rim. That's not where women excel. It's not what they do best. Their game is different. And there's absolutely nothing wrong with that.

Why do we insist that women repeat the same stupid mistakes men do, and then call it progress? Men do really dumb things. We see weapons of mass destruction where there are none. We over-emphasize sports. We place athletic achievement ahead of academic achievement. We spoil and pamper child athletes and then complain when they act spoiled and pampered as adults.

Do militant feminists realize just how stupid we are? No, I'm being serious. For the life of me I can't figure out why any woman would see equality in being anything like me or any of my friends. We have no relationship skills and even less patience. We're walking, talking, eating, somewhat educated weapons of mass destruction. We pretty much tear apart everything good in our life out of fear that the good things are really bad things just waiting to get us.

It's a vicious cycle that women would be wise to avoid.

(And, yes, I have major drama in my life right now. I just wanna curl up in a fetal position and tell my mama all my problems. But she doesn't care. She probably doesn't like me, either. I didn't mean that mama ... if you're reading. I know you love me ... I think ... Don't you? Call me on my cell.)

Where was I? Oh, the dunk contest.

Why can't we just celebrate Candace Parker's game? She has lots of game. She's not the best girls' prep basketball player because she can dunk. She has soft hands, quick feet, great vision, a nice shooting touch, good moves around the basket. That was good enough to make Larry Bird a superstar. It should be good enough for Candace Parker.

She shouldn't have to hide her eyes in a horrible Dee Brown dunk imitation to be considered a star.

■

Golfer caught in bad lie gets what he deserves
April 24, 1997

*In 1997 21-year-old Tiger Woods blistered Augusta
National with a record 18-under to become the first
African-American to win a major. Following his victory,
PGA Tour veteran Fuzzy Zoeller made some disparaging
remarks towards Woods. In the weeks that followed, a
national debate ensued over Zoeller's comments and the
reaction to them.*

In a just world, the goal is not to treat everyone the same.
It is to treat everyone fairly.

Consider that for a moment. Fairness superseding same-
ness. Identical treatment not equaling fairness or justice.

If you can understand that life tenet, then you can understand, accept and appreciate what is happening to professional golfer Fuzzy Zoeller.

On the Sunday that 21-year-old Tiger Woods became the
first black man to win the Masters, Zoeller made some
racially insensitive remarks about Woods to a group of
reporters. Zoeller referred to Woods as "that little boy" and
urged Woods not to serve fried chicken and collard greens
or whatever "they serve" at the Masters champions dinner.

(As the defending champion, Woods will select the menu.)

Zoeller has since said he was joking, claiming that everyone on the PGA Tour knows that he's quite a prankster, comedian,

Fuzzy Zoeller's "apology" to Tiger Woods rang hollow to a lot of people and wasn't well received by many in the media.

funnyman. Kmart Corp., Zoeller's primary golf sponsor, didn't buy Zoeller's alibi and on Tuesday ended its relationship with the one-time Masters champion.

On Wednesday, Zoeller held a face-saving news conference, where he apologized to Woods, announced that he was pulling out of the Greater Greensboro Chrysler Classic and that he wanted to meet with Tiger Woods.

Zoeller is obviously fearful of being Jimmy The Greek-ed or Al Campanis-ed — run out of professional sports because he was ignorant enough to spew his racial prejudices in front of a live microphone and camera.

And many of you are sympathetic toward Zoeller, especially those of you who haven't seen the videotape and therefore foolishly believe that Zoeller was joking.

You think American culture has set up an unfair double standard.

Charles Barkley, a black basketball player, can jokingly say, "I hate white people" and there are no repercussions. Tiger Woods, a black and Asian golfer, can rattle off several racially insensitive jokes to a magazine reporter in an off-the-record conversation and there are no repercussions. While Zoeller, a white golfer, says "boy" and jokes about black people's love of soul food and there are a multitude of repercussions.

Zoeller is a victim of political correctness gone amok, you say.

That line of thinking is unsophisticated and immature.

Zoeller is being treated fairly, not the same as Barkley or Woods or any other athlete who makes a stupid statement.

Zoeller is a victim of his own ignorance, bigotry and avoidance of common sense.

The fact is that America has a despicable history in regard to how white people have treated America's black citizens.

That history has deservedly given greater weight to ethnic slurs spoken by American white people directed at American black people.

That's not a secret. We all know the history and the rules.

Fuzzy Zoeller knew this when he opened his ignorant mouth. Just as Barkley knew that his marriage to a white woman and his close business and personal relationships with white men would allow him to get away with publicly joking about hating white people.

On the Saturday that Woods took control of the Masters, Tom Watson remarked on television that Woods was a "boy among men" and that Woods was showing the men how to play. It was a poor choice of words. But if you saw Watson say it on TV, you knew he didn't use the word "boy" because of Woods' race. It was a statement about Woods' youth.

There was absolutely no uproar about Watson's statement. Watson, a white golfer, was treated fairly, not the same as Zoeller.

Kmart rightfully doesn't want to be represented by an athlete who has a problem with a 21-year-old black man dominating golf's most prestigious event.

Zoeller's Wednesday apology rang as false to me as Roberto

Alomar's belated apology to umpire John Hirschbeck. Zoeller was motivated by fear and money Wednesday — fear that he won't make any more money from major corporate sponsors. That would only be fair.

■

In every case, one word simply inexcusable
June 8, 1997

This is one of the most original and daring columns in Jason's career. In this piece Jason tackles a delicate issue and takes a stance that makes so much sense you wondered why the column hadn't been written a million times. This piece took a sports issue and turned it into a much larger social issue.

B ryan Cox, the outspoken, highly volatile NFL linebacker, is like a majority of people who keep popping up on daytime television in the 1990s. He doesn't belong. Unsophisticated and inappropriately educated, he's a frequent interviewee only because he's easy to exploit.

If not for the millions of dollars the Dolphins and the Bears dumped in his pocket, Cox would be the perfect example of the kind of person who has made millionaires of Ricki Lake, Jenny Jones, Geraldo and countless other talk-show exploiters of the poor, uneducated and simple-minded.

(And yes, I'm aware Cox graduated from Western Illinois University. A diploma alone does not reveal a person's level of intelligence or education.)

I mention all of this because about a week ago Cox appeared on ESPN's "Up Close" — the sports version of daytime gab, where athletes routinely reveal their inner-most thoughts while posturing handsomely for the benefit of their wives, groupies and potential groupies — and, to no one's surprise, Cox made some outrageous assertions.

"If some white guy I don't know calls me a nigger, I'm going to kill him," Cox proclaimed while staring indignant-ly into the eyes of white interviewer Chris Myers and as ESPN's ratings jumped a point.

Cox made that statement in the middle of explaining to Myers why he feels it's appropriate and acceptable for black people to use the N-word.

"I'm using it as a positive thing... " revealed Cox, who

admitted that he allows his children to use the N-word.

"To me, I'm not degrading myself."

Interesting. And, given Cox's well-documented, erratic behavior, it would be easy to say "harmless." But it's not.

Too many black people agree with Cox's assertion for it to be harmless.

Plus, ignorant, unrebuked, public statements on an issue as sensitive as race are rarely harmless.

Recent events involving high-profile sports figures — O.J. Simpson, Fuzzy and Tiger — have brought the race debate into the forefront of our discussions about sports, making many people uncomfortable, and some people cry foul about a double standard.

Well, there should be no double standard about the use of the word "nigger."

Both black and white people, for different reasons, should not tolerate the use of the N-word.

An explanation is unnecessary for why non-black people should not use the N-word.

Black people should not use the word because of the psychological toll it has and does extract on American blacks.

When you hear a Bryan Cox or any black person attempt to justify the use of the N-word they are speaking out of ignorance.

They have no understanding of the purpose for the creation of the N-word or how the N-word is serving that purpose perfectly in the 1990s.

The N-word is not unlike the word "gook," the pet name our Armed Forces called the Vietnamese during the Vietnam War. Our military adopted the word "gook" because it understood that our soldiers were going to participate in inhumane acts against the Vietnamese people. It is easier on a soldier's mind to drop napalm on "gooks" than on human beings.

It also is easier on the mind to enslave, whip, lynch, rape, maim, segregate, under- and mis-educate a group of "niggers" than a group of human beings.

That's why hundreds of years ago, slave-makers gave humans of African descent the pet name "nigger."

And that's why today — as black people have embraced and popularized the use of the N-word and seem to relish using it publicly, privately, in our sleep and on every rap song invented — black people live in total fear of each other, in total fear of the black-on-black crime wave.

If you look at it objectively, as we have embraced this word over the last 10 to 15 years, we have more and more tended to treat each other as the "niggers" we so gleefully call ourselves.

Bryan Cox and the inventors of the N-word must be proud.

■

Decision not to play is right one
September 14, 2001

Following the September 11, 2001, attacks on the World Trade Center and the Pentagon, commissioner Paul Tagliabue announces that the NFL would suspend play for one week.

We don't need any diversions. We need to think and pray and meditate and re-evaluate.

I want to congratulate NFL commissioner Paul Tagliabue for canceling games Sunday and Monday and for providing other American sports leagues the courage to follow suit.

Our attention doesn't need to be diverted. By canceling games we have surrendered nothing important to the terrorists who destroyed the World Trade Center, the Pentagon and our sense of safety.

This is not a time for senseless arrogance. This is a time for reflection and contemplation. Our world has changed. Life as we have known it here in America has changed.

After suspending play for one week the NFL returned to action on September 23, 2001. As the Chiefs hosted the Giants a group of firefighters passed an American flag through the crowd.

So let us surrender our silly distractions this weekend. Let's give the terrorists that insignificant victory and use this weekend to prepare for the war.

There's only one way for the terrorists to win. They cannot stand up to our military might. They know that. The terrorists don't win if we sacrifice a weekend of entertainment or endure security inconveniences at airports. The terrorists win if we surrender to our feelings of racism, if we split along ethnic lines and repeat the mistakes of the past. The terrorists win if we allow our thirst for revenge to control our actions rather than the thirst for peace.

The war is being waged in our minds and hearts. Do we allow our hearts and minds to fill with racism and revenge? Do we pressure our president and our leaders to react irrationally?

If we do, then we've let the terrorists win.

I don't want any diversions. As much as I love football, I didn't want to see the Chiefs play the Seahawks on Sunday. I want to reflect, meditate and pray. Our leaders will take their cues from us.

It's no different than what we just witnessed with Tagliabue and the NFL. Pro football is king in this country. Tagliabue's courage affected the rest of the sports world. President Bush needs to know that we have the courage to support whatever decision he might make.

If he senses that our racism and desire for revenge is out of control, he will feel pressured to react in a way that satisfies those emotions.

Patriotic Muslim and Arab Americans died in the World

Trade Center. We need to think about that this weekend. We need to remind ourselves that Muslim and Arab Americans were as repulsed by the attacks Tuesday morning as the rest of us. We need to talk to our children and loved ones about that.

We can't afford to repeat the mistakes of the past. We violated the rights of Japanese Americans during WWII, locked them in camps, and we were forced to pay them reparations years later. The terrorists win if we do that again.

And whatever military action we might take must be a step toward long-term peace, not a step toward extracting revenge.

Revenge is a great weapon in the world of sports. It might inspire the Chiefs to beat the Raiders later this year. In every other endeavor, revenge is a deadly boomerang. Again, the terrorists and their supporters are no match for our military. Their only real weapon against us is men filled with revenge willing to carry out suicide attacks of random terrorism.

I'm not nearly wise enough to know what President Bush should do. I'm going to support whatever decision he and his Cabinet make. But I want to be informed. I want to spend time thinking about the significance of these events. I'm going to take that time this weekend. I'm glad I won't have to deal with the distraction of football or baseball or NASCAR or Tiger Woods. We spend too much time in a fantasy world already. The realities that visited us Tuesday morning will haunt the rest of the world for years.

We've been lucky.

Now that our luck has run out, we should act accordingly. Let's use this weekend for mourning, reflection, prayer and fellowship with family and friends.

■

CU scandal misses big picture
May 30, 2004

*During the spring of 2004 the University of Colorado foot-
ball program was rocked by numerous allegations of rape,
sexual abuse, and the use of strippers and alcohol to entice
recruits. Following an investigation by an independent
panel, head coach Gary Barnett and athletic director
Richard Tharp both retained their positions, despite heavy
criticism in the panel's report.*

No one has the right to complain that the University of
Colorado did nothing in the wake of its just-completed
two-month investigation into the school's sex-and-alcohol
football recruiting scandal.

You have no right to be disappointed that football coach
Gary Barnett and athletic director Dick Tharp retained their
jobs. Firing Barnett and Tharp would have accomplished
nothing. It wouldn't even come close to addressing the real
issue.

Big-time college football and basketball specialize in recruiting athletes who are unprepared socially and academically to fit in at the universities they represent on the field
and court. In order to get the athletes to overlook this obvious fact, athletic programs have cultivated and maintained
a recruiting culture that relies on sex and intoxicants to help

the athletes, particularly black athletes, forget that they'll never be comfortable or totally accepted on campus.

This recruiting culture was pervasive throughout college athletics long before Gary Barnett and Dick Tharp stepped foot on Colorado's campus. And this culture will live on as long as college coaches and universities believe it is impossible to win a conference or national championship without recruiting and educating athletes who are unprepared socially and academically.

It's called exploitation.

There are profound lessons to be learned from what has transpired at Colorado. Unfortunately, we have lazily danced around the real issues.

"There is that perception out there that CU is the No. 1 party school.... Everybody has known about that; it's the big elephant in the room that no one wants to talk about," CU Regent Tom Lucero was quoted as saying in a wonderful article in Saturday's Rocky Mountain News. "But the other elephant sitting in the room is the race issue; everyone wants to tiptoe around it."

Yep. Two issues kept creeping up in the Colorado investigation: booze and race. They're the peanut butter and jelly of sports. Inseparable. Strippers, hookers and Barnett stole most of the headlines, but booze and race — although ignored — were never out of the mix.

Colorado's black athletes feel isolated (and targeted) on a campus and in a city that is overwhelmingly white. It took DNA test results to clear two Colorado football players of a rape allegation issued by a white student who said she was too drunk to remember whom she went home with.

All she said she could remember is that the men were big and black.

On a campus with more than 20,000 students, Colorado has fewer than 500 black students. Forty percent of CU's football team is black, which is roughly 40 players.

Approximately one out of every 11 black students on CU's campus is a member of Barnett's team.

Black athletes on white campuses have been complaining about racial inequity for as long as I can remember. When I was a football player at Ball State in the late 1980s, it was an almost weekly occurrence to gather around and moan about how the campus wasn't set up for us, the black students. We had a black student council, a black Ms. Ball State, a black This and a black That. None of it made Ball State feel like Grambling. It was rather stupid. I remember asking my teammates and classmates: "Did they tell us this was a black campus when they recruited us? Did they tell you this was Eddie Robinson North on your recruiting trip?"

No.

"So why are we upset now when we get here and find out you can't get your Murray's grease, a wave cap and Jet magazine at the university bookstore?"

The universities do not falsely advertise. They are what they are. And in their athletic programs they rely on athletes who are too immature, too unsophisticated and oftentimes — on their recruiting trips — too buzzed and too aroused to care whether a particular university best serves their academic and social needs.

Most black athletes would be better served at a historically black college. A black student is six times more likely to graduate from a HBC than a predominantly white school.

The education is just as valuable; many of America's great black leaders graduated from HBCs. Attending school at a HBC does not mean a graduate would have difficulty assimilating into America's workforce. Does Oprah Winfrey have any trouble assimilating?

Another myth is that black athletes need the exposure of attending a "big-time" school if they want to make it to the pros. Tell Jerry Rice and Steve McNair that. Tell LeBron James and Kevin Garnett and countless major-league baseball stars. Pro scouts scour the globe looking for athletes. If a pro league can find you in high school, you can rest assured scouts will find you on a college campus. It doesn't matter what level of competition you play against or how many times your school has been on TV. Professional leagues draft on potential.

This is not a pro-segregation rant. I'm not for segregation in any form.

I am for people making informed decisions and doing what's best for them. If universities would like to eliminate some of the embarrassing corruption in college sports, school presidents should quit allowing their institutions to recruit athletes — black, white, brown and yellow — who don't fit in academically or socially.

And athletes should take their marketable talents to schools that want them and are best equipped to nurture and support them academically and socially. Everyone would benefit from that.

■

Tillman a reminder of what sacrifice is
April 24, 2004

Following the September 11, 2001, attacks, Pat Tillman
of the Arizona Cardinals left his NFL career behind and
enlisted in the Army Rangers. On April 22, 2004, Tillman
was killed in action at the age of 27 while serving in
Afghanistan. He was posthumously awarded the Silver
Star for his actions.

Obviously, Pat Tillman's life was a lesson about sacrifice.
But we realize it even more now, now that Tillman has
made the ultimate sacrifice.

Tillman, an Army Ranger and former NFL player, gave his
life fighting terrorists in Afghanistan. When Tillman, 27,
walked away from a $3.6 million contract and joined the
U.S. Army after the 9/11 tragedy, he became a symbol of
American patriotism. We celebrated his sacrifice.

I'm not sure we understood it. We should now.

I'll never forget Pat Tillman. He taught me the true meaning of sacrifice. Sacrifice should hurt. Sacrifice should
make you uncomfortable. My generation, we've had it so
easy. We've never been asked to make any real sacrifices.

We have no real concept of commitment or discipline or sacrifice.

Most of today's professional athletes believe sacrifice is attaching their name to a charity, giving money to a cause or showing up at an autograph session for kids. Those things don't hurt.

True sacrifice hurts.

Take the politics of the war on terrorism out of the debate — whether you agree or disagree with President Bush's policy is irrelevant — and Tillman is no different from Martin Luther King Jr. and Nelson Mandela, men who became heroic symbols of sacrifice in pursuit of freedom.

We can't put Tillman on too big a pedestal.

His sacrifice is not greater than the sacrifice of the other men and women who have given their lives in Iraq and Afghanistan. But there's always someone who stands as a symbol. Martin Luther King Jr. wasn't the only man or woman to lose his or her life in the fight for equal rights in this country. Nelson Mandela wasn't the only man or woman jailed in the fight against apartheid.

Some people may be offended that so much attention will be given to Tillman's death. Don't be. It's not a slap at the other soldiers. Tillman just happened to have the most unique story. He turned his back on the American fantasy. He was young, good-looking, intelligent and on the verge of becoming a millionaire. He had everything our freedoms promised, and he chose to defend those freedoms rather than drown himself in their excesses.

Tillman is a hero. We can't celebrate him too much. We can't talk about the lessons he taught enough.

He served his beliefs with humility. He refused all interviews. He refused preferential treatment. He sacrificed until it hurt.

I spent much of Friday afternoon trying to reconcile the fact that I feel the same way about Pat Tillman that I do about Muhammad Ali. Think about that one. Ali went to court to avoid military service in 1967. He participated in flamboyant and cocky news conferences. Ali never saw a microphone he wouldn't blab into. After a three-year fight, the Supreme Court eventually ruled in Ali's favor.

You would think it would be impossible to find common ground between Tillman and Ali. Not for me. They both made tremendous sacrifices. Ali, as heavyweight champion, would have received special treatment in the military. He probably never would have seen combat.

By fighting the draft, Ali risked going to prison, forfeited his heavyweight title, lost the prime years of his fight career and became one of the most hated men in America at the time.

Ali and Tillman followed their beliefs. Ali refused to go to Vietnam for religious reasons. Tillman joined the military because Americans were attacked on American soil.

Both men are heroes. It feels as if it's been 30 years since a professional athlete has actually stood for something besides a new contract. Athletes have long played a significant role in American society's evolution. Ted Williams probably would have surpassed Babe Ruth as the home-run king had Williams not served in the military. Jackie Robinson jump-started the civil-rights movement. John Carlos and Tommie Smith used the Olympics to make a point about American inequality.

Now let's add Pat Tillman's name to the list of big-time athletes who made a real difference, and let's hope we don't have to wait another 30 years for the next one.

■

KU soccer coach must take blame

May 14, 2000

*In the spring of 2000 a pair of Kansas football players
were accused of sexually assaulting a member of the
women's soccer team. After consulting with her coach
and then-football coach Terry Allen, the victim chose not
to involve the police and instead let Allen discipline the
players. In October 2000 the athletic department issued
a report recommending changes in the handling of sexual
assault reports; no charges were filed.*

Kansas football coach Terry Allen is feeling the heat that
should be directed at KU soccer coach Mark Francis.

Last week Allen was forced to stand before his peers and
apologize for his involvement in the sordid handling of
allegations by a women's soccer player that she was a
victim of sexual battery by two KU football players.

The woman claims that in a private meeting with Allen
and Francis, just a few days after the alleged assault, Allen
persuaded her to allow him to discipline the players in
exchange for the woman not reporting the incident to
police.

According to the woman, the players were made to run stadium steps. That light punishment provoked her into taking
her allegations to Lawrence police nearly two months after

the alleged assault. Allen claims his discipline extended beyond that but has yet to reveal what the additional punishment involved.

OK, so we've established that Terry Allen isn't the most sensitive man in America. But what football coach is? My contention is that the system failed when Francis advised his player to meet with Allen.

Under no circumstance should the woman have ever met with Allen.

A coach's first instinct is — and should be — to protect his player. Allen, while wrong, acted to protect his players. Can we say the same about Mark Francis?

"I gave her good advice," Francis said when reached in his office Friday afternoon. "The initial advice I gave her was that you need to go to the police, and in addition to that you need to talk to Terry Allen."

Good advice?

Only if Terry Allen is the woman's father or a sexual-assault counselor or Dr. Laura.

The University of Kansas pays Terry Allen to win football games and promote a positive image of the football program. He's not assigned to meet the needs of KU women's soccer players.

That responsibility falls on Mark Francis' shoulders.

Based on his handling of this situation, I don't think Francis is qualified for the job.

This is my own personal pet peeve. I don't think any man should be the head coach of a women's team.

"I don't think that's an issue at all," Francis said when I broached this topic with him.

Of course it's an issue. Let's suppose a member of Marian Washington's women's basketball team had accused two football players of sexual battery. Do you think Marian Washington would have said, "You need to talk to Terry Allen"?

The mere suggestion is laughable.

Now let's suppose that the women's soccer team was coached by a first-year coach who happened to be a woman. New on the job and faced with a major crisis, whom do you think a female coach would've turned to for counsel on how to handle a situation so potentially explosive?

Marian Washington or Terry Allen? Associate athletic director Amy Perko or Terry Allen?

Aw, but boys will be boys. They'll look toward each other
to solve their problems and girls' problems, too.

In our sexist society we think nothing of it when men coach
women. We ignorantly think it's a sign of equality. But
we'd think it was incredibly foolish if women began coaching men in the same proportions.

I'm not trying to suggest that every male coach would have
handled this situation as Francis did. Neither do I believe
that women should coach women simply because they
would handle sexual-assault cases properly. Women make
mistakes, too.

My belief is — and I don't think I'm out on a limb here —
that women understand women better and are more natural-
ly equipped to handle a number of issues relating to women
athletes. And I realize there are a number of men who excel
at coaching women.

But Francis' action in this instance repulses me and is a
good example of how out of place men are being in charge
of women. Francis has made everyone — the woman, the
players and the Kansas athletic department — a victim.

It seems the woman was inclined to handle this situation

out of court. Now she's likely to have her personal life picked apart. Her desire seemed to be to have the players punished — significant suspension, serious counseling, heartfelt apology — not jailed or criminally labeled as sex offenders.

Mistakes happen in college environments, where youth and drinking too often collide. These mistakes shouldn't haunt the students for the rest of their lives.

The adult who made the biggest mistake in this situation is Mark Francis. He should suffer the harshest penalty.

In the Moment, Part 2: The Greatest Disappointments and Tragedies of the Last Decade

Magic of dream deferred will be hard to recover
December 6, 1998

In 1998 it appeared Kansas State was ready to reach the summit of the college football world. Having beaten Nebraska for the first time in three decades, the Wildcats finished the regular season 11-0 and won their first Big 12 North Division title. They headed to the Big 12 Championship game in St. Louis to face Texas A&M, where a victory would put them in the BCS title game.

ST. LOUIS - Today is not the day for criticism. Kansas State's football doubters will have to wait until tomorrow to have their say.

Today is a day for sorrow, a day to lament what slipped away.

Kansas State's dream season turned nightmarishly ugly Saturday afternoon inside St. Louis' TWA Dome.

The BCS was supposed to keep the Wildcats out of the national-title game, not Texas A&M, not Branndon Stewart, not Sirr Parker.

Aggies 36, Wildcats 33.

The Big 12 championship, an undefeated season, a trip to the Fiesta Bowl and a possible national championship slipped wickedly through the Wildcats' hands Saturday.

Parker did the final deed, catching a third-and-17 slant pass from Stewart and dashing 32 yards for a touchdown in the second overtime. Parker ran through the arm tackle of a K-State defensive back, and with one knee on the ground, he lunged the ball across the goal line. The referee signaled touchdown.

Just that quickly, K-State's dream season turned ugly.

"The pain that comes from this comes from the emotional investment," K-State coach Bill Snyder said. "The greater the investment, the greater the pain."

Sirr Parker celebrates after scoring the tieing touchdown in the fourth quarter of the 1998 Big 12 Championship game. Parker would later score the winning touchdown in overtime.

There's a lot of pain in the state of Kansas today.

The Fiesta Bowl table was set for K-State earlier in the day when Miami's Hurricanes pulled off an improbable, come-from-behind upset of UCLA. At that time, it seemed that

Snyder had done the impossible.

He appeared to have taken college football's worst pro-gram to the mountaintop. All the Wildcats needed to do was beat a very beatable Texas A&M squad, an outfit that lost to Texas a week ago.

They couldn't do it.

They couldn't do it even though Texas A&M coach R.C. Slocum made tactical error after tactical error. In the third quarter, he tried for a two-point conversion from the 8. It failed. Slocum passed up fourth and goal from the 1 and kicked a field goal in the first overtime, seemingly giving up A&M's best chance to win.

The Wildcats should have won Saturday.

Quarterback Michael Bishop had a splendid day running and passing the football. He nearly had the perfect day.

I say nearly because his fumble late in the fourth-quarter let Texas A&M back in the game. It allowed the Aggies to force overtime. The Wildcats led by eight at the time. The Aggies scored quickly, converted a two-point conversion and survived Bishop's Hail Mary pass that was caught by Everett Burnett at the A&M 1.

That's how close the Wildcats came to playing for a national championship.

This was K-State's year to be national champion.

The Wildcats won't be because their defense could never fully stop Stewart, Texas A&M's quarterback. Bishop's fumble was costly. But K-State's suspect pass defense lost this game.

Two weeks ago, Missouri quarterback Corby Jones exposed K-State's weakness in its pass defense. Stewart did what Jones could not do, however. Stewart closed the deal.

He threw three touchdown passes. He repeatedly made big throws on third and long.

He stole K-State's national-championship season.

Today is not a day to rip the Wildcats, who obviously benefited all season from playing a weak schedule. They barely dodged death against Nebraska and Missouri. Their record against top-10-ranked opponents is 1-35; the only victory came against an overrated 1995 Kansas team.

Saturday, A&M ruined what had been a perfect K-State season, a season that made you believe anything is possible. It made you believe that a driven, single-minded coach could lift a moribund program to the ultimate greatness.

Maybe Snyder can still do that. It's just that next season, next time, it will be harder to dream, harder to believe.

Bishop made the Wildcats believe in miracles.

I'm not sure whether there are any miracles left in Manhattan, Kan. This might be as good as it gets.

■

There had better be some changes made
January 8, 1996

The Chiefs dominated the regular season during the nineties, but all those victories never amounted to a Super Bowl appearance. In 1995 the Chiefs went 13-3, had home-field advantage through the playoffs, and looked destined for their first Super Bowl trip in 25 years. Instead, on a cold January day at Arrowhead the Indianapolis Colts ruined Kansas City's dream and turned the name "Lin Elliot" into a swear word.

This one is unforgivable.

You don't throw away home-field advantage to the Indianapolis Colts, a team that sneaked into the playoffs with a sandlot quarterback (Jim Harbaugh). You don't throw away a 13-3 regular season to the Indianapolis Colts, a mediocre team playing without its No. 1 player (Marshall Faulk).

You just don't do what the Chiefs did Sunday at Arrowhead Stadium.

They committed an unforgivable crime.

They gave away the Super Bowl without putting up a good fight.

The Chiefs — from team President Carl Peterson to place-kicker Lin Elliott — can't walk away from Sunday's embarrassing 10-7 loss to the half-baked Indianapolis Colts just with hurt feelings.

Jim Harbaugh walking off the field after the Colts stunned the Chiefs at Arrowhead Stadium in 1996.

There must be repercussions.

Let's start with the easy part. Elliott should be waived. Today.

Elliott's removal from the roster — and the Kansas City area — would start the healing process with fans. His removal is actually a month overdue. He should have been cut after he botched two extra points and a field goal at Oakland on Dec. 3.

Elliott's three missed field goals (35, 39 and 42 yards) Sunday — including a wide-left boot with 42 seconds remaining — sabotaged another outstanding effort by the Chiefs' defense and a last-gasp rally engineered by backup quarterback Rich Gannon.

Lin, I checked with the airlines Sunday night. You can get a one-way flight on American Airlines to your hometown of Waco, Texas, for $116. The flight leaves at noon. If you need a ride or a loan, call me at 234-4869. It's no problem.

Now, for the hard part. And it really isn't all that difficult — not if egos and pride are placed to the side. (I hope you're reading this, Carl.)

American Airlines also has a flight to San Francisco that leaves at noon. It's a bit more expensive, $243. But I'm willing to foot the bill for this one, too.

Steve Bono, the finicky eater and even finickier passer, should be on that flight. Actually, his wife and kids should be on it, too, because his return is unwanted.

Bono, the 10-year backup, as Chiefs starting quarterback was an interesting experiment. Unfortunately, it's an experiment that failed. His grades were borderline during the regular season, and Sunday he flunked the final exam, throwing three interceptions in his first playoff test.

"You can't evaluate just one game," said Peterson, who signed Bono to a three-year contract extension before the beginning of this season. "You evaluate an entire year. Steve's had a tremendous first full year."

That's untrue.

Bono has been erratic all season. He finished the season as one of the AFC's least-efficient passers. His horrid performance Sunday — 11 of 25 for 122 yards — had nothing to do with his 79.5 regular-season rating (12th in the AFC).

In reality, Bono had little to do with the Chiefs' 13 victories. He simply has been at the wheel of a successful truck that's powered by a resilient defense, a dominant offensive line and the NFL's most intelligent running back, Marcus Allen.

Bono isn't good enough to lead a team to the Super Bowl. He was the on-field weak link in the Chiefs' chain. And according to Peterson and Coach Marty Schottenheimer, making the Super Bowl is the Chiefs' only objective.

One last repercussion before I let you go.

Offensive coordinator Paul Hackett must be replaced (or Marty's authority to change Hackett's calls must be revoked). He and the Jerry Rice offense can head back to the West Coast. The offense has been a failure in Kansas City.

And Sunday the Chiefs' play calling was ridiculous. After the first quarter, two things were obvious: 1. Bono was out of sync. 2. The Chiefs' running game was in sync.

Despite those two obvious factors, the Chiefs, who never trailed by more than three points, often threw the ball when they should have been running.

"I couldn't believe it when they started throwing on first down," Colts safety Jason Belser said.

I couldn't believe it when the Chiefs threw to little-used fullback Tony Richardson on third and 1 at the beginning of the second half. Richardson, who has never caught an NFL pass, dropped Bono's low throw.

It was one of many unforgivable mistakes.

■

March sadness:
Missing ingredient a mystery
March 22, 1997

The 1996-97 Kansas Jayhawks will be remembered as maybe the best team to not go to a Final Four. After starting the season as everyone's pick to win it all the Jayhawks entered the NCAA tournament with a 32-1 record and a No. 1 seed.

BIRMINGHAM, Ala. - Something was missing.

We may never know what, but after Friday night's heart-breaker it's clear that something was missing from this group of Jayhawks, the college basketball team that looked so perfect, the college basketball players every mother wanted their daughters to bring home.

Arizona 85, Kansas 82.

Let's call it more March Sadness.

That's what the Jayhawks have experienced at the conclusion of each of the last four seasons. Kansas teams that seemed built for the Final Four have died in dramatic, gut-wrenching fashion in the NCAA Tournament, always a game or two short of the Final Four, college athletics' grandest event.

Friday night, at Birmingham's Civic Center in the semifinals of the Southeast Regional, Kansas' season expired. A flurry of three-pointers could not save the Jayhawks. They had fallen too far behind and had expended too much energy slicing a 13-point deficit.

Ranked No. 1 for most of the season, the Jayhawks fell to the Pac-10's fifth-place team, Arizona's Wildcats.

And with that, the Jacque Vaughn, Scot Pollard, Jerod Haase and B.J. Williams era ended at Kansas.

It concluded without a Final Four appearance. The class that clearly brought coach Roy Williams his greatest joy is the first Williams graduating class to leave Kansas without a Final Four appearance. In fact, it's the first Kansas class since 1981 to leave Lawrence without a date in the Final Four.

Something was missing.

"You know, I hope not," Williams said. "As a coach I'm going to do a lot of soul-searching myself to see if there's something missing from Roy Williams. I'd like to think there isn't. ..."

"I'm going to keep knocking at the door, and one of these days we're going to knock the sucker down."

He'll knock with a vastly different group next season.

The group that had it all is no more.

This season Kansas had the consummate point guard in Vaughn, the nation's top power forward in Raef LaFrentz, a small forward with the ability to take over the game offensively in Paul Pierce, an experienced center who could dominate defensively in Pollard,

After a shocking loss to Arizona in the 1997 NCAA tournament Paul Pierce and Raef LaFrentz head for the locker room. Neither of the All-Americans would ever play in a Final Four.

leadership and all-out hustle in Haase, the best bench in the country in B.J. Williams, Ryan Robertson, Billy Thomas and T.J. Pugh, and a coach, Roy Williams, who has duplicated Dean Smith's record-setting system.

All that and no Final Four.

It doesn't seem fair, particularly when you factor in the intangibles: the character and class and uniqueness of this group of players.

Vaughn may be the next Bill Bradley, a wonderfully gifted

basketball player with the intellect to ascend to greater heights off the court. If not Vaughn, then Haase.

And will Kansas or college basketball ever produce another Scot Pollard, a player who can paint his fingernails, wear goofy sideburns and propose marriage to his girlfriend at center court in front of 16,000 witnesses without the world concluding that there's something wrong?

Nope. These Jayhawks had it all. Yet something was missing.

It wasn't outside shooting. The Jayhawks had plenty of that this season and Friday night, nailing 10 three-pointers.

It wasn't a "go-to" player. LaFrentz and Pierce solved that problem. Friday night Pierce (27 points and 11 rebounds) played like the best player in college basketball.

And it wasn't toughness. Yes, LaFrentz and Pollard were outmuscled and outplayed in the first half Friday night. But it would be simple-minded to say those two weren't tough this season just because they had off games Friday.

What was missing from these Jayhawks is impossible to identify. Maybe all they were missing for four years was luck. Whatever it was, I'm sure it is irrelevant in the game of life. But it would have made all the difference in the NCAA Tournament.

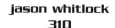

Forget the loss: Missouri prefers favorable future

November 13, 1997

Missouri teams have earned a reputation for coming so close to pulling off major upsets only to watch buzzer beaters and bad calls rip victory from their hands. In 1997 the MU football team appeared to have beaten Nebraska, which would go on to win the national title.

COLUMBIA - This Missouri heartbreak is different from the others.

The Fifth-Down loss and the Tyus Edney shot, the two sporting events most closely identified with Missouri athletics in the 1990s, were pretty meaningless. Missouri was nothing more than a faceless, anonymous speed bump on Colorado's dash to the 1991 football national championship and UCLA's run to the 1995 NCAA basketball title.

Those gut-wrenching, out-of-nowhere defeats said little about the Tigers, except that they were cursed with incredibly bad luck.

Saturday's Nebraska heartbreaker meant something, however. It wasn't a fluke.

Coach Larry Smith's Tigers outplayed then-No.1-ranked

Nebraska for 59 minutes and 59 seconds — or up until the moment Nebraska receiver Matt Davison dived from nowhere, cupped the ball and threw another dagger in Tiger hearts — and if the two schools lined up this Saturday, the Tigers would be competitive with the Cornhuskers again.

Football is back at Missouri.

That's what Saturday's 45-38 overtime finale shouted.

"We've turned the corner," said Missouri coach Larry Smith, whose 6-4 Tigers face Baylor on Saturday. "Now one season doesn't make a comeback, but it can be the steppingstone for a complete comeback."

This Missouri heartbreak is so different from the others.

While the rest of this area — and a significant portion of the football-loving country — is still re-living and re-playing Nebraska's stunning victory, Smith and his Tigers are moving ahead.

There's no time for the Tigers to think about the unfairness of Nebraska's victory, which was the product of an illegal kick, or to dream about where they'd be ranked if not for the final play of regulation.

Smith has learned from Missouri's previous heartbreaks.

"You can't dwell on it," he said after a crisp two-hour practice on Wednesday. "If you dwell on it, it could bury you for the next 15 years. You've got to move on and play the next game. We've got to beat Baylor. That seventh victory is really important. We've turned the corner, but we want to get all the way around the corner."

On Friday the Classic Sports Network is going to re-broadcast Nebraska-Missouri: "The Flea Kicker," the game so tantalizingly good that it reached legendary status in less than a week.

"Nobody on this team is going to watch," Smith declared. "We're not going to watch that stupid game."

For too many years, Missouri celebrated its close defeats, wallowed in its near upsets. Smith won't let it happen. That's why this heartbreak is so different. It signifies a new attitude at Missouri.

The Tigers have too much to look forward to to relive an old nightmare. Ever since their embarrassing 41-11 loss at Kansas State a month ago, the Tigers have played like a top-25 team. A bowl invitation is a certainty if they knock off 2-7 Baylor.

And next year?

Who knows?

MU quarterback Corby Jones will start the season as one of the leading contenders for the Heisman Trophy. Since K-State, he has been the best option/throwing quarterback in the country. "Our best players stepped up their play after K-State," Smith said. "Our quarterback jumped up his."

The Tigers lose just one of their starting offensive linemen. Seven of their defensive starters will return. The attention generated from their three-game winning streak and near upset of Nebraska has top-notch high school recruits responding differently to Missouri recruiting phone calls.

This Missouri heartbreak is going to lead to something very big, very heartwarming if you love old Mizzou.

■

Carver is bright light to so many
September 14, 1999

*Kansas City native Randie Carver was well on his way
to a successful boxing career before tragedy struck on
September 12, 1999. During a fight against Kabary Salem
at Harrah's North Kansas City Casino, Carver was repeatedly head-butted and collapsed in the tenth round. He was
rushed to the hospital and underwent emergency brain
surgery. Carver never regained consciousness and was
on life support until he died on September 14 (this column
appeared in The Star on Tuesday morning, a couple of
hours before Carver was pronounced dead).*

All Monday afternoon Randie Carver's loved ones trudged
through North Kansas City Hospital in groups of twos and
threes.

Young, old, black, white, rich, poor, male and female paced
the waiting-room area, broke down in tears, laughed hysteri-
cally, traded stories, clasped hands in prayer and replayed
Sunday evening's tragedy.

As Randie Carver desperately fought for his life, the many
lives he touched converged just a few feet from his hospital
room, hoping that some miracle would make Randie open
his eyes.

Who could blame them?

Randie Carver has always made people believe in miracles. Randie Carver has always been a symbol of what is right about this world.

"I don't know anybody who didn't like Randie," sighed Jeff Brown, Carver's lifelong buddy.

Carver's sister, Fannie Paul, added: "There was nothing Randie wouldn't do for anybody."

God blessed Kansas City with Randie Carver. Fate cursed Carver with the ability and discipline to box.

Sunday evening, 10 rounds into a nationally televised dirty brawl with an Egyptian mauler, Carver collapsed in the ring. Several times he violently rolled over and tried to spring to his feet, making it to his knees before falling unconscious.

A neurosurgeon performed emergency brain surgery on Carver late Sunday night, opening a section of his head to relieve the pressure and reduce the swelling of his brain.

If Carver, 25, survives, he'll never be the same.

He may never talk or walk again.

"I wish my boy had never chosen this profession," Brown said. "I used to ask him all the time, 'Of all sports, why this one?' "

It's a good question.

Professional boxing is beneath Randie Carver. Prize fighting is for men with no options. It's for men with rap sheets and wicked intentions.

Randie Carver has neither.

Randie Carver is the nicest person you'll ever meet. He's the son every man dreams about raising. He's the boy every mother wants their daughter to bring home. He's what we want professional athletes to be — humble, sincere, loyal and honorable.

"This kid is the greatest role model I've ever seen as an athlete," said Tony Holden, Carver's fight promoter.

"Randie was the good son," admitted Paul. "He always wanted to make things better. He stayed out of trouble."

Carver, a Westport High graduate, is a hard-knocks kid who refuses to live the hard-knocks life.

Born into poverty, one of nine children raised by his mother, Barbara, Carver weathered the scars of seeing two brothers and one cousin jailed and one brother murdered execution-style in his sleep.

Carver got involved with boxing at the age of 10. He won a national Golden Gloves title. He should have been a U.S. Olympian.

He should have never turned to professional boxing. He received a Kauffman Foundation college scholarship.

He didn't need boxing. He was bright and articulate. But boxing got a hold of Carver at an early age and never let go.

"At 13, he told me that boxing was going to be his way out of the ghetto," said George Smith, Carver's trainer and surrogate father. "He was a kid who was supposed to fall through the cracks. But he didn't. He didn't because at an early age he was focused. Not only did he know what he was going to do, but he followed through on it.

"Randie's the closest friend I have in this world. There's no one who can fill his shoes."

Smith is right in so many ways. Randie Carver is a bright light in Kansas City's inner-city community. He gives his time to schoolchildren unconditionally. He is the bright light in his family.

"Everybody looked up to Randie," said Jana Clark, a Carver family friend.

We must pray that never changes.

■

A hero's farewell:
Yes, cynics, that's what Thomas deserves, and here's why
February 15, 2000

On January 23, 2000, Chiefs' linebacker Derrick Thomas was involved in a one-car wreck that killed one of his passengers and left Thomas with severe spinal cord injuries through his neck and back, leaving him paralyzed. Thomas was airlifted to Miami, underwent surgery, and was preparing to begin rehabilitation. On February 8 while in a hospital a large blood clot caused Thomas to go into cardio-respiratory arrest and he died. Prior to his funeral Derrick Thomas' casket lay in state at Arrowhead Stadium.

There's nothing wrong with celebrating Derrick Thomas as a hero.

Along with the deep outpouring of sorrowful emotion among Chiefs fans concerning Thomas' one-car accident and subsequent death, there has been a silly, steady undercurrent of cynicism, jealousy and judgmental disapproval of the way Thomas conducted his life.

The argument goes that we in the media are holding up Thomas as a saint and perfect role model for kids when in reality he was far from it. The argument further states that we in the media have been reluctant to point out that Thomas' recklessness and poor decision-making caused his death and the death of his good friend Mike Tellis.

The argument has been expressed to me in e-mails and voice-mail messages. My sports editor, Mike Fannin, has fielded several complaints from Star readers. I've heard it on my radio show.

All of you are wrong.

Thomas' failings don't diminish him as a hero. They only reveal him as just as human and just as flawed as the rest of us.

I've never bought into the theory of athletes as role models.

It's stupid. It sends a ridiculous message that somehow some wealthy jock your son or daughter has never met has more influence over your kids than you (the parents) do. That's just not true.

Derrick Thomas had a responsibility as a role model to his seven children, his brothers and sisters, and the kids he came in regular contact with through his Third and Long Foundation.

For everyone else, Thomas was nothing more than an example.

As the Chiefs open the 2000 regular season, a B-52 bomber flies over Arrowhead in a tribute to Derrick Thomas

Thomas was an example that adults could point to and say, "Hey, regardless of the situation, regardless of the fact that your father has died or isn't here, you can still become someone special in this world."

He was an example adults could point to and say, "If you're ever blessed with great wealth, don't forget to turn back around and offer someone less fortunate a helping hand."

Those are the two things we know most about Derrick Thomas. He overcame incredible odds to become someone special in America. And when he became special, he remembered to share his blessings with others.

That's why there's nothing wrong with celebrating Derrick Thomas as a hero. He was a hero to me.

His devotion to his charitable foundation was real. It wasn't a public-relations ploy. He lent much more than his name to the foundation. The time I spent with Thomas and Neil Smith visiting sick children at local hospitals was one of the most moving experiences of my life. You have no idea how mentally and physically grueling it is to visit sick child after sick child, hospital after hospital, until you've done it for 3 1/2 hours. It takes a toll.

I can offer you no opinion about what kind of a father Derrick was to his children. That's none of my business. That's between Derrick, his children, the mothers of those children and God.

A big NFL contract and fame don't entitle us to know everything about a celebrity. Plus, Thomas' personal relationships were irrelevant to us. He was never an elected official. His personal dealings never caused him to run afoul of the law.

Thomas was a football player and a philanthropist. He never portrayed himself as a social angel. He never hid where he liked to socialize. He was a flawed human being, just like you, who was in the process of evolving beyond some of his flaws.

As for Thomas' role in his demise and the demise of Mike Tellis?

I don't think anyone felt worse about that than Thomas. Of course, he should have been wearing a seat belt. Of course, he should have allotted more time to get to the airport.

These truths are self-evident.

And so is this one: Derrick Thomas deserves to be remembered and celebrated as a hero.

He influenced our lives positively. He made living here a richer experience. He had a good heart. He cared about people. He faced up to his mistakes like a man and accepted the consequences of his mistakes, even when he thought those consequences were too harsh.

■

Incomplete: This drama didn't deserve lousy ending
January 5, 1998

For most NFL teams a 13-3 record and home-field advantage through the playoffs is a recipe for success. But for Kansas City it has become a sign of disaster. In 1997 the Chiefs shocked much of the league by rolling up the best regular season record in the AFC, and many thought it would be their chance to finally break through. Instead for the second time in three years fans at Arrowhead watched a playoff victory slip away as the Chiefs failed to execute in the closing moments.

It was everything you expected. Except the ending.

The mother of all NFL playoff games, Kansas City vs. Denver, knotted your stomach, raised your blood pressure and pushed you to your emotional breaking point. It made you sit on the edge of your seat, cross your fingers and take your phone off the hook.

The Chiefs vs. the Broncos for the right to meet Pittsburgh for the AFC championship gripped you, captivated you, and in the end it shocked you.

John Elway flicked darts. Neil Smith harassed the quarterback. Elvis Grbac found Tony Gonzalez in the back of the end zone. Andre Rison webbed the ball. Denver's Terrell Davis rumbled for 101 yards. Marty Schottenheimer coached dangerously and foolishly. So did Denver's Mike Shanahan.

It was a defensive struggle, but entertaining nonetheless. The AFC's two best teams scratched and clawed each other for the better part of three hours. You couldn't take your eyes off the action.

It was everything you wanted. Except the ending.

The ending was a bad joke. A really bad joke. Fuzzy Zoeller on HBO's Def Comedy Jam would elicit more laughs.

Broncos 14, Chiefs 10.

More than 30,000 spectators stood silently frozen inside Arrowhead Stadium 10 minutes after the Chiefs and Broncos had cleared the field. The ending, so abrupt, so unexpected, so disturbing, left you dizzy and confused and wondering how a magical 13-3 regular season could dissolve so wretchedly once again.

One moment, the Chiefs were confidently driving for a game-winning touchdown — or at least a series of game-deciding plays from the red zone. The next, they were out of timeouts, standing in disarray at the Denver 20 and adlibbing a last-ditch, ill-fated bomb to Lake Dawson into double coverage.

And you were left remembering Indianapolis, Lin Elliott and 1995.

"I never thought it would happen again," said Kansas City running back Kimble Anders, recalling the Indianapolis playoff debacle that ruined KC's last 13-3 regular season. "I would have bet everything I owned on us winning today and next week. This one hurts so much more."

This ending was crueler than even Elliott's last field-goal attempt.

Five plays and one timeout in 2 minutes.

That's what the Chiefs' offense managed with the game on the line, with their season hanging by a thread, with their reputations at stake.

It would be an insult to Mao Tse-tung to call Kansas City's 2-minute offense a Chinese fire drill. Let's just say Richie Cunningham accomplished more in the back seat of a '57 Chevy in 2 minutes than the Chiefs did on Sunday.

Ted Popson refused to run out of bounds and stop the clock. Grbac couldn't hear quarterback coach Mike McCarthy's signals.

The Chiefs looked silly, poorly coached and cursed.

"They were hurrying, they were scattered, they were rattled," Denver linebacker Bill Romanowski said later.

"We just didn't play smart," Grbac said after surfacing from the Chiefs' eerily silent and bitter locker room.

It all falls in the lap of Schottenheimer, the Chiefs coach for the last nine years. John Elway, the quarterback who allegedly has Schottenheimer's number, didn't beat Schottenheimer this time. There was no Drive, no Fumble.

The Chiefs beat themselves.

Special-teams captain Greg Manusky wiped out a Kansas City field goal with a holding penalty. In the first half, Grbac never challenged Denver's defense by throwing down field. And early in the fourth quarter, facing fourth and 6 from the Denver 31, Schottenheimer gave punter/ holder Louie Aguiar the option to run around right end on a fake field goal.

All 53 Broncos, plus their coaching, medical and training staffs, were expecting the fake.

"I should have called it off and taken a delay of game," Aguiar said. "They lined up differently than what we had studied on film all week."

Before the game, Schottenheimer promised to continue with his 1997 gambling ways. But you don't double down when the dealer's showing an ace. It opens the door for critics. And leaves a coach with a 5-11, no-Super Bowl playoff record defenseless.

"I can't argue with them right now," Schottenheimer help-lessly said when asked how he would respond to the critics who believe he can't win in the playoffs. "I can't argue."

Neither can he deny that the offense he invested in so heavily during the off-season — signing Grbac, Rison, Popson and Gonzalez — let him down in the biggest game. The Chiefs scored just three more points Sunday than they did in their 1995 playoff loss to the Colts. And little-used, minimum-wage receiver Joe Horn made the Chiefs' biggest offensive play, hauling in a 50-yard Grbac bomb.

Progress?

Well, they did look better scoring 10 points than they did scoring seven.

"I said many, many years ago," Schottenheimer said, turn-ing introspective, "when I first started in coaching that at the end of each day I would walk to my mirror and look in it and ask, 'Marty, is there anything else you could have done in this day to enable you and your football team to be successful?' And if the answer was 'No, you've done what you needed to do,' then I rest easy."

Schottenheimer's rest won't be easy for a while. This ending was too bad.

■

Don't show your face again in this town
April 17, 2003

Most KU fans thought they had finally seen the last of the "Roy Williams to North Carolina" story when Williams chose to stay at KU in 2000. But after North Carolina forced out Matt Doherty following a disappointing 2003 season, the Jayhawks made their run to the national title game with rumors swirling that their coach would soon be departing. Jason blamed Kansas grad Dean Smith, who reminded Jason a year later that he still remembered this stinging column that appeared on ESPN.com.

LAWRENCE, Kan. -- Dean Smith is the only man more disliked here than Roy Williams.

Smith's name is basically a curse word around the Kansas campus, where Smith earned a degree and played on a national championship team, and where Williams built a basketball dynasty.

Traitors.

That's the prevailing sentiment around town since Williams announced Monday that he'd prefer to return to his North Carolina Tar Heel roots rather than complete his Kansas legacy. Williams, the feeling is in Lawrence, caved to Smith's emotional pleas, which included telling Williams that he was the "only one who could salvage" the Carolina program.

"People can't believe Roy has the nerve to show up at the banquet," said Larry Sinks, 40, a Lawrence businessman.

The Jayhawks will celebrate their Final Four season tonight with their annual season-ending banquet. Williams returned to Lawrence yesterday afternoon and plans to crash the banquet. Williams wants to make peace with his players and Kansas fans.

Ike might have a better chance of making up with Tina.

Kansas fans are irate, not just because Williams left, but because of the way he has conducted himself during his Chapel Hill press conference and subsequent national TV interviews. KU fans believe Williams' overzealous praise of recruits David Padgett and Omar Wilkes during interviews is nothing more than Williams trying to subtly suggest to the high school seniors that they ask Kansas for a release from their letters of intent.

"I feel bad for KU's veteran players," said Dru Fritzel, a KU season-ticket holder since 1985 and a Lawrence businesswoman. "Roy talked and talked about those two recruits and hasn't really said anything about the kids who helped him get to the championship game. I feel sad for them."

Sinks has sold close to 5,000 anti-Williams, anti-North Carolina T-shirts out of his Victory Sportswear store since Williams began re-flirting with UNC. Sinks can't keep up with demand for "Benedict Williams" shirts.

"I started at 5:30 a.m. and it was pretty much non-stop business until I left around 6:30 p.m.," said Sinks, a long-time Kansas basketball supporter. "Most Kansas fans are kicking themselves. They're wondering, 'Why did we put Roy on a pedestal like he was God? We were so naive.' "

Jayhawks fans put Roy on that pedestal because they thought he was their version of Dean Smith, who twice rebuffed overtures from his alma mater to return to Lawrence. Now Kansas fans don't want Williams or Smith anywhere near Lawrence.

"I've lost a lot of respect for (Smith)," said Rob Farha, owner of the popular KU tavern The Wheel, where Williams regularly ate lunch. "Dean has shown no loyalty to Kansas. Roy is 52. If he wants to answer to Dean Smith the rest of his life, I guess that's his business. But Roy had his own thing here."

Sinks added: "Dean is the worst guy of the whole bunch. He better never show his face at KU again. I can't tell you the words and the things I've heard said about Dean Smith around here."

Traitor. Selfish egomaniac.

If Roy Williams is telling the truth, and it was indeed another gut-wrenching decision between Kansas and Carolina, then I blame Dean for all the pain that Williams and Kansas fans are experiencing right now.

And Williams is in a lot of pain. He broke down in tears on my radio show Wednesday morning and in a private conversation. He knows there's no explanation for his decision that would provide Kansas fans adequate comfort. He can't even make himself completely comfortable with the decision.

At one point Wednesday morning, he claimed he was no different than any person "on your street who has switched jobs in the last 15 years." The truth is Roy Williams always preached that coaching at Kansas was far more than a job. He asked players and fans to emotionally invest in the Kansas basketball family.

You can change jobs with very little pain. You can't desert your family without creating a lot of pain.

Dean Smith should know that better than anybody. He should've respected the basketball family that Williams built at Kansas and counseled his coaching pupil to stay with his new family. But Smith's ego wouldn't allow that. It wouldn't allow Roy to build a family that rivaled Dean's. Dean is the only real winner in all of this. Roy flushed 15 years of hard work and damaged his relationship with countless former Kansas players.

"I am very upset," Scot Pollard, a Sacramento Kings forward, told the Lawrence Journal World. "I feel the guy made the choice three years ago, and the reasons he gave three years ago have not changed. ... If he thinks I'm going to North Carolina for an alumni reunion, it will not happen."

KU players accepted Williams' invitation to view him as a father figure. Now those players will be denied enjoying the kind of relationship Williams has enjoyed with his Carolina basketball father for all of these years.

All because Dean Smith wants North Carolina to be a slave to his legacy.

Williams, a good man caught in a horrible situation, will regret this decision for the rest of his life. Even several UNC national titles under his guidance won't ease this pain.

■